Country Blacksmithing

Country Blacksmithing

by Charles McRaven

PHOTOGRAPHS BY **Linda Moore McRaven and the Author**

DRAWINGS BY **Chandis Ingenthron and the Author**

1817

HARPER & ROW, PUBLISHERS, New York

Cambridge, Hagerstown, Philadelphia, San Francisco,
London, Mexico City, São Paulo, Sydney

To Bill Cameron, the best blacksmith's helper I ever had.
And to "Shad" Heller, who taught me more than anyone else.

By the same author

BUILDING THE HEWN LOG HOUSE

BUILDING WITH STONE

FIRST EDITION

Designer: Linda McRaven

Library of Congress Cataloging in Publication Data

McRaven, Charles.
  Country blacksmithing.
  Includes index.
  1. Blacksmithing. I. Title.
TT220.M13   682'.0973   80-7876
ISBN 0-06-014870-5
ISBN 0-06-090870-X (pbk.)

81 82 83 84 85 10 9 8 7 6 5 4 3 2 1

Contents

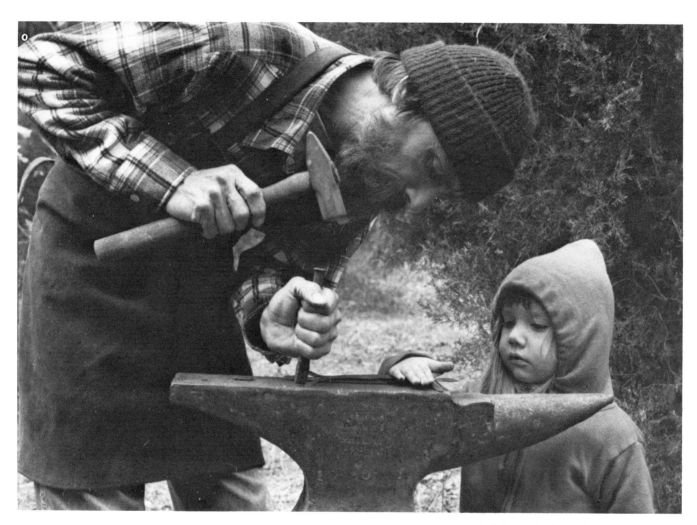

While a blacksmith shop isn't ordinarily the place for children, here three-year-old Amanda holds a piece to be worked cold, the veining of wrought-iron leaves.

Introduction

Country Blacksmithing is meant for the man or woman who is working toward independence: on an acre or two of deep woods or on an overgrown farm, in a hand-built cabin or in a van or in a falling farmhouse that is feeling again the touch of hands that care.

It is significant that most of the other books on blacksmithing are by artists; working iron can certainly be an art. But here it is treated as a craft, one of survival, one of skill applied to the business of modern pioneering. You can go a little way back to the earth or a long way—whatever your needs and abilities—but mastering the iron on the anvil is such a basic craft that it will draw you farther than most others. In learning to work the black metal, you commit yourself to a level of independence that thumbs its nose at the world of plastic and of throwaways.

Each piece you forge will be the only one of its kind, a creation so personal and so enduring that it makes your statement of self-sufficiency all over again. Each tool, each working mechanism of hammered iron puts your stamp one more time on that bit of universe you are making so much your own.

The instructions in this book are basic and practical for you as a homesteader, and the projects are among those I have done again and again in setting up places in the country four times, over the years. I've found that, along with the woodworking skills, shaping iron can put you farther toward independent living than any other craft. You can conceivably make anything of iron or steel that can be made, although it may take you longer.

You may become something of a purist in working iron, using the most primitive tools and procedures to produce work that will give you the deep satisfaction of having done it by hand. Or you may find for your purposes that the time you can allot to smithing may demand shortcuts, powered tools and machinery, and more of the very equipment that made the basic smithy largely obsolete. But as long as you heat a piece of iron and shape it to your purpose, you are carrying on an ancient craft that helped civilize the world. This craft can make your homesteading a richer experience, it can save you time and money, and it will certainly root you deeper in the land.

Buck Mountain Creek
Albemarle County, Virginia
January 1981

CHAPTER ONE

The Pioneer Smith

Setting up your forge on your own homestead will parallel so nearly the experience of the pioneer blacksmith coming into the new country that comparisons are inevitable. You may already have your place established—cabin, clearing, garden—and you will no doubt be a settler first and a blacksmith second instead of the other way around. You may wind along your woods road in a wheezing pickup truck or a station wagon with your anvil sitting solid back there and your tools clinking on the way home. But it's all so nearly the same. The early smith made settlement possible; in this day the craft can make it so much better, so much nearer the independent ideal.

Let's now look in on a pioneer blacksmith, your counterpart of two hundred years ago, and listen for his voice, and the echoes of his old tools.

The pioneer smith came into the new country much as did the other early settlers—with axe and rifle and his family, if he had one, jammed into a single wagon—up the forks of wilderness creeks following the search for land. He was most often a farmer, too, and the hunger for new territory drove him as it drove the others west from the Carolinas, from Virginia, and from the Northeast.

But this man had in his wagon a treasured anvil, a hammer or two, an assortment of scraps and bits of iron, and a head full of answers to the mysteries of working the black metal. He'd served a long apprenticeship in a shop in the Eastern settlements, and maybe as a journeyman in a wagon works or a musket factory.

And his wagon, laden with the barest needs for a frontier home, moved slowly with its weight of iron toward the beginnings of a settlement. A primitive gristmill might be set up at a big spring, its timbers raw and new among the fresh stumps and the falling water. These two craftsmen often located together, the smith and the miller, to serve the scattering of backwoods cabins hewn from the crowding forests.

The smith would find a welcome among the hunters and the settlers in the creekside clearings. He would often be taken into an already crowded cabin with his family so he could get his shop put up sooner. His house could come later, with a community log-raising marked by hard work, good food, courting, games, and raw, new whiskey from yet another craftsman's still.

Under a shelter of some kind, the smith would build his forge, often of stones laid up with clay between, with a passage for air from the giant wood-and-deerskin bellows. The primitive forge might have a flue or might not. It might have an iron firepot cast back East or one of his own forging, riveted together. Or he might use a grate of iron bars set into the stonework, and no firepot at all.

Tongs would perhaps have been brought West, but most likely space in the wagon was reserved for tools that were harder to make. Taps and dies for threading handmade bolts were rare and prized, and a smith was well equipped if he possessed these.

Iron was in short supply, and often steel was available only by close trading or by the slow process of case-hardening in the forge. The frontier smith traded habitually, for food and supplies, for worn wagon tires and pieces of horseshoes to be shaped into the needs of the new community. Charcoal was his fuel, burned in sealed kilns, unless he was in coal country.

And he made the shoes for the settlers' horses, and the chain for their harnesses, and mended the broken iron braces for their wagons. He hammered a new flintlock for a long rifle, or straightened its barrel, bent

An early country blacksmith's work, this double hook with upset ornamental ends was on a New Hampshire farm wagon.

This nicely primitive chain hook strap is one of two on an Ozark mountain farm sled. The shape, hammered from old wagon tire, kept the chain from slipping out when slack.

perhaps in a border brawl. The smithy became a stop along the lengthening wilderness road West, where the ravages of travel were patched and mended and the iron made whole again.

It's hard to imagine how little the smith had to work with. In a situation where a simple bar of iron was almost nonexistent, he might hammer half horseshoes, worn in two at the front, into nail rods for nails for a split shake roof. Or shape a salvaged brace from a splintered wagon that could go no farther into an auger, case-hardening it into crude steel. And this same brace could have been part of a wagon tire before, or a worn axe, and something else before that.

The smith made it all, including household fixtures like swinging fireplace cranes, skillets, and pots; forks, spoons, and knives; and the files to sharpen the knives. He made saws for the carpenter, hammered and hardened; mill picks to dress the miller's stones; and iron collars for the wooden shafts in the mill.

When iron became more common, he poured the bearing metal for the sawmill shafts and hammered buggy axles and candle holders. As plows evolved to steel from the old wooden ones, the circular saw came into being, and as the steam engine came, the tasks of the smith changed. As the age of machines grew, he became a specialist, building and repair-

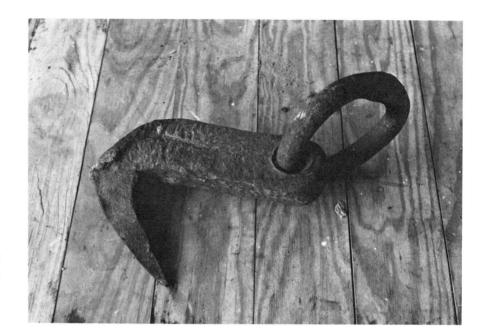

A hand-forged log-skidding hook from the mountains of Kentucky. The point was driven into the log, with a chain attached to the ring. Two were used together, as a sort of free-form pair of grabhooks. This was a gift from Bill Chatfield, whom I helped restore a log house, and for whom I forged two sets of andirons.

ing them, until those same machines finally forced the smithy to close, ushering in a century of stamped-out, cheapened iron.

The frontier smith might trade for crude steel of a doubtful carbon content from back East, or he might venture into foundry work to produce his own steel if he had the knowledge and equipment. Most likely he would place a bar of wrought iron in a case of iron or clay, packed with ground-up bone or old dry leather or even hair. This case went into the forge along with the pieces he was shaping, and stayed red-hot for many hours. Gradually the red bar of iron inside absorbed carbon from the organic material around it as the material charred. The surface of the bar became steel, deepening as the treatment continued. When the bar was forged, the hammering spread the carbon steel throughout the iron bar to raise the overall content. This was case-hardening, a make-do way to produce a very limited amount of steel.

Sometimes the knife or axe or chisel was forged first, then case-hardened so that only the outer layer was steel. As the tool later wore and was sharpened, the steel gave way to soft iron again. In the back country today there are still a lot of old-timers who believe that you will eventually wear or sharpen an axe or knife down past the good steel to soft metal underneath.

What actually often happens is that finely made cutting tools are hardened and tempered only near the edges to guard against breakage. The steel is the same throughout, and a worn tool can be rehardened and tempered over and over. Cheaper tools are hardened only to a medium degree throughout. They don't break, nor do they hold the cutting edges of the finer pieces.

The old blacksmith was often accorded an esteem far out of proportion to his knowledge. The term "black metal" refers only to iron, as opposed to tin or silver or pewter, white metals. But there has always been a mystique to mastering the iron that placed the smith's work just a step from black magic. Many an old codger can tell you of a "real" smith from the days of his youth who could and did work magic at his forge every day. Mysterious steels that could be contorted and return to their shapes, knives so sharp they'd cut into wood when laid on it, tempering fluids that imparted properties to the steel that defied wear.

Of course, the old smiths did nothing to discourage these beliefs. Some tempered in ox blood, some in mercury, for the supposed super qualities they gave the steel. There's a story of one illiterate smith who bought at great price a recipe for a quench guaranteed not to crack the steel and to make it harder than any other. He had the written formula filled by a chemist, who was evidently in on the swindle. After many years of successful but costly use of the magic liquid, the smith revealed the formula to a trusted associate who could read. It called for so many parts aqua and so many of chloride of sodium. That story's been around among smiths for a long time.

Today we know that the liquid for quenching steel has only one function: to cool steel of a given carbon content faster or slower. Three basic liquids are used. Most smiths agree that plain water is fastest, for a harder steel, but its fast cooling can crack steel. Salt water, that mysterious formula, slows cooling somewhat, for a tougher steel that is not as hard. Oil tempering is the use of an oil quench that cools slower, for less hard-

A neat bit of early forgework, part of a bucksaw turnbuckle. It was made by hammering the loop of half-round iron, then forge welding the ends, rounding, and threading the left-handed threads for this half of the turnbuckle.

13

ness in the steel and more toughness. It all has to do with the boiling points of the liquids, nothing else.

On the other hand, you can read in half the books on the subject today that salt water gives the hardest quench, plain water is next, and oil is for toughness. My advice invariably is to try it yourself when you get to hardening and tempering steels. I will confess that I never use salt water at all, getting exactly the results I want, even in delicate tool-making and knife-making, from plain water or oil quenching. But lots of modern smiths quench only in salt water, and their method works for them.

The few early smiths who really knew this weren't about to admit it publicly. Their reputations rested on their supposed knowledge of the mysteries of the iron, and this set them apart from the ordinary farmer or laborer. If more smiths had indeed known what was really going on in their often hit-or-miss craft, it would all still have been a grand ongoing joke.

The amazing thing is that early smiths were able to do as well as they did to keep the settlers supplied. In fact, folks just were used to living with iron that wore out soon, with steel with brittle places in it that broke, and with workmanship that, while not perfect, was a vast improvement over their own abilities. The demands of frontier life were simple, and the smith's work seldom had to be of machine-shop caliber to meet those demands.

Most farms and plantations had their own shops, and took care of most of their own needs. The commercial smith was usually located in a settlement, where other folks tended to specialize and didn't have the time, inclination, or ability to do their own iron work. The farmer-smith shod his horses, made his chain and hinges, sharpened his plows, and

An early forged rope hook, probably shaped this way to attach to a taut line, keeping it secure, as it slid along it.

Singletree from New England, of wrought iron, with decorative snake hooks. Hook shape kept the trace chains from falling out.

steeled his axes as far as he was able, turning to the specialist in the village for the jobs he couldn't handle.

Many an old homestead in the country today has a small forge back among the junk in the barn, and maybe an anvil half covered with hay. Grandpa did his own blacksmithing, and a lot for the neighbors, but Papa went off to town, and nobody's touched that stuff for years.

The day of this writing I have just returned from a visit upcreek a mile to the home of a new settler from Chicago. Terry Burke was leveling the stony hillside in the woods outside his new house when he struck iron. It turned out to be a buried anvil, and more digging uncovered several sets of tongs, a froe, and some horseshoes. He called me to find out if I knew of a blacksmith shop there, because he'd found no trace of a building.

Well, this is only a couple hundred yards off the old stagecoach road around the mountain, at a spring where the little branch of a creek gets going. Most of the tools suggested a horseshoeing operation, so the earlier settler probably did some business with travelers on the stage road. There were traces of a bridge across the branch, and faint traces of a road up out of the hollow: The smithy probably collapsed with age or burned down many years ago. I'm trading a hand-forged broadaxe and some other homesteading tools for the forged Peter Wright 113-pound anvil. Terry will split shakes with the froe, just as his predecessor on that site did.

This hollow, a tangle of second-growth woods when we came in 1972, apparently held a dozen or more cabins, and the old smith probably served them all, along with the transient trade. A washed-out mill dam farther downcreek suggests another early craftsman. And the old log church still stands on down where our branch meets a larger creek.

Your own experience setting up your place in the country will parallel that of the early settler, in many respects. So will that of establishing your smithy, whether exclusively for your own farmstead use, to supply your rural neighbors as well, or even for commercial projects. You probably won't want all primitive hand tools, like the craft centers try to use, but if you're out past electricity, this is the course you'll have to follow, more or less.

I use a combination: A hand drill press and a hand blower on the forge, but an electrically powered trip-hammer, and sometimes an acetylene cutting torch and an arc welder. I make my own tongs and chisels and punches and lots of other tools, but I buy a hammer head at a junkshop, and rarely pass up any cheap piece of blacksmithing equipment, even though I could make it myself.

But whether or not you are a modern-day pioneer, whether or not you use powered equipment, whether you are located in the woods or the suburbs, yours is a kinship with the frontier blacksmith. The hammer striking the forge iron, hot on the anvil, has never changed.

CHAPTER TWO

Getting Your Tools Together

Setting up your forge and acquiring the tools you'll need is an exercise in invention. What you can't locate at auctions, garage sales, or in junkyards, you can make yourself—and the more complete your shop, the easier it becomes to make more tools.

The forge is of course the key to the shop. It has to be simply a contained fireplace with an air-blast channel (tuyere) (too-yair) up through it. It can have a clinker-breaking device, an ash dump, and a flue to carry off smoke. A clinker is a chunk of metallic slag melted out of the coal. The forge can be iron or masonry or both. It can have a bellows or blower powered by hand or motor. New forges are available, but they are prohibitively priced, and you should learn early to fabricate your own equipment. Let's look at some alternatives.

I use three forges. One is a simple pan-type farrier's forge with just a heavy screen at the bottom through which the air comes up, an ash dump, and a small sheet-iron hand blower, all set on pipe legs. It's light, and handy for transporting to craft fairs and workshops. I have worked steel into a 9-pound wood-splitting maul with it.

The second forge is of my own construction, using a small but sturdy cast-iron blower, a cast firepot and tuyere with triangular clinker breaker and ash dump. The fireplace is steel plate, curved, with low sides and a cutout for long pieces. It's on three legs of recycled reinforcing rod. This forge is heavier than the pan forge, and can handle bigger work.

The third forge has a heavy, deep cast-iron firepot set in stonework with the slitted round tuyere/clinker breaker and ash dump. It's charged by a separate Champion 400 hand blower on its own stand, bolted to a concrete slab. This forge is four feet square, with a reinforced concrete fireplace cut out for long work. We heated a 70-pound anvil on it to harden it on one occasion, so it can handle heavy work. Its stone side forms part of the low stone wall of one side of my shop.

My brother John has a small forge made from an automotive

(top left)
A simple forge for most jobs. First, two pairs of legs of recycled reinforcing rod are welded together.

(top right)
The legs are welded to a piece of flat steel plate about 8 inches square.

(lower left)
A piece of 2-inch water pipe is welded to the bottom of the plate, and a hole cut in the side, where a piece of 1¾-inch conduit is welded.

(lower right)
An automotive brake drum is centered over the plate, holes are bored to bolt through, or it can be welded in place. A grid of holes is bored to open into the pipe up from below. This is a top view.

18

brake drum, charged with a small sheet-iron hand blower. He does all the forge work for his farm, and a limited farrier business on it. His blower, attached to a pipe with ash dump, came from a junkyard for $10.

My sheet-iron blower was also $10, my small cast one $12.50, both from farm sales. From a friend I bought my large blower, with a Peter Wright 160-pound anvil, for $100. The heavy firepot came from a junk-shop for $15, the small one from an auction for $3.00. The original farrier's forge, with damaged rachet blower, was $15 at a junkshop.

I'd advise starting small, with a forge of your own devising, to avoid spending much money. You will soon find your own particular needs, and can be on the lookout for better equipment, or make it yourself. A large brake drum has a good shape for a small pan forge. Braze legs onto its outer rim (it's cast iron, so brazing is the safest way to go). Brazing is welding with brass, so the cast won't crack as it cools. If welded with

The forge nearly complete. The broken handle of a junked blower was welded, and will get a wooden grip. The ash dump can be a threaded pipe cap, or a weighted hinged trapdoor. A light steel rod brace strengthens the blower mount, bolted to it and welded to the cast-iron brake drum with bronze or nickel rod. Care should be used not to let the fire burn shallow, or the plate base of the forge will burn or melt. This forge took less than four hours to build; materials cost less than $5.00.

arc or acetylene, the cast iron should be preheated, then allowed to cool slowly afterward. Also, slant the legs of this forge outward to keep it from tipping, since it is so light in weight. Next, bolt a disc of steel plate over the big hub hole in the bottom, through the wheel lug-bolt holes. Bore ¼-to-⅜-inch holes in a circular pattern in the center of this plate to let the air come through and for the ash grate.

Next weld or braze a 2-inch water-pipe tee to the plate disc, and thread a piece of pipe 12 inches or so long from it for the blower. Then you can use a pipe cap or collar and plug at the bottom to seal it. It is easily removable to dump ashes. Weld a bar across the plug to make it easier to unscrew.

Shop around for a small hand blower. They can often be found rusted up, or with the handles broken, very cheap. The fan will usually be sheet iron and some of the blades be bent, but you can straighten them. It's harder to weld or braze replacement blades on and keep the fan in balance. You can soak the bearings loose with penetrating oil.

I recommend a hand blower because you have complete control over the fire. An electric blower will free your other hand, true enough, but you will burn lots more coal with an electric blower, and a moment's inattention will let you burn carbon steel or thin mild steel, which you'd have had your eye on if you were hand cranking.

A leather bellows is the oldest form of air blast we know of. Al-

Masonry forge firepot, showing tuyere/clinker breaker inside, with handle weighted for proper air blast, air inlet, and ash dump at right. Cutouts at left (really the top, in use) allow stock to go lower in the fire.

A Champion 400 blower on a stand, which I use with the big firepot in my masonry forge.

Handmade, four-foot bellows, belonging to Dr. David Morris, of Earlysville, Virginia. This is a double-action bellows, with the center panel held stationary, mounted horizontally. The missing handle pulls the bottom panel up to force air out the nozzle and up into the top chamber, where a weight pushes it out after the handle is released, freeing both the smith's hands.

dren Watson goes into great detail on the construction of the bellows in his *Village Blacksmith.** The bellows takes a lot more room than the gear blower, but has more nostalgia connected with it. It was most often used where the blower wasn't available, as when a pioneer built his charcoal forge out in the wilderness. The double bellows does keep on blowing for some time after you let go, however, which frees hands for tricky things like forge welding.

If you brace your blower pipe to the lip of the forge pan, you can mount the blower directly on it. My pan forge is done this way, with a bolt through the pipe. The midsize forge blower is mounted on a plate welded to the pan lip, with flexible automotive exhaust pipe down to the air inlet.

There are disadvantages to a simple forge like this. First of all, you have to heap coal up to get a deep fire, and it's easy to burn out your plate grate. Also, if there is no clinker breaker, you must take the fire apart every time to clean it before you forge weld, since there must be no clinkers for this operation.

Otherwise, this lightweight forge will get you started and allow you to do most jobs around your farmstead. Keep the forge clean and out of the weather. Rain on burned coal will seep sulfuric acid from the sulfur down and eat out the bottom of your forge very soon.

Next is the anvil, and few tools are so hard to find. Like the forge, which can be bought new, the anvil is available, but it's from $2.00 to $4.00 per pound, currently. Used ones are over $1.00 a pound just now, with really good ones $1.50 or so. There are two kinds of the London pattern anvil we're most familiar with. One is the cast-steel anvil still manufactured, which is one piece, with the top hardened by chilling as it is cast. Cast anvils tend to ring nicely, which means next to nothing when applied to their efficiency. (A brittle cast bell rings even better, but you can't hammer iron on it.) The only part of the anvil that should be hard is the top surface, or face. When inspecting a used anvil, look for chips or cracks in the top, which I find to be most common in cast anvils. We'll talk about repairing them later.

The other kind of anvil is the forged one, which was formed in three pieces: the base, body, and top plate. These were welded together, sometimes as a technical school project, with strikers (blacksmith's helpers) hammering the heavy sections at welding heat. The top plate was of steel, the lower parts of iron. The anvil was then chilled and tempered, affecting only the face, to harden it.

These anvils are rarer today than cast ones, and represent a high achievement of the metalworker's craft. I find that these anvils seldom ring sharply, being mostly soft iron, but are quite as good to work with as

*Aldren A. Watson, *The Village Blacksmith* (New York: T. Y. Crowell, 1968).

HARDENED FACE OR PLATE

PRITCHEL HOLE

HARDY HOLE

TABLE OR STEP

HORN

WAIST

LONDON ANVIL

the best cast anvils. Common faults are a chipped or a broken face, or even a separation of the weld of part of the plate.

You will hear much about the ringing of the anvil. The best one I ever used rang not at all, but had a perfect face that was hard enough to bounce the hammer nicely. It was a forged anvil, which I borrowed for years, and I recall it fondly. But it rang not once.

The overall hardness of a piece of steel or cast iron causes it to ring when struck. Cast bells ring nicely. So does brittle cast steel, high in carbon. And while it is true that an anvil that rings nicely is good to listen to, it just might break under a heavy sledgehammer blow someday. Don't make the sound your only criterion.

Any anvil will wear with use, so you may well find a specimen with a wavy face, or one sloped off sharply from drawing and scarfing (procedures we'll explain later), the smith having used the same side over and over. I work from every side of the anvil, so can often use a worn anvil, concentrating my work on the good surface that is left.

Refacing an anvil is always possible, though the old surface may have to be built up or milled down to be flat enough to weld a new plate onto. If it's to be milled or ground flat, the face should be annealed, which means heating the anvil redhot. A big brush fire with logs and

The London anvil. This is a forged anvil, showing clearly the joint at the welded hard plate, or face, on top. It's also welded at the narrow waist. At left is the horn; at right the tail, with the square hardy hole and smaller round pritchel (punch) hole. The step at left center is not hardened, being used for cutting, with hammer and chisel.

stumps in it will generate enough heat, then the anvil should cool very slowly. Afterward you can grind it flat with a portable "sidewinder" body-shop grinder, or have it milled.

If there's enough plate left on a forged anvil, or if yours is a cast one, the plate can be rehardened after milling. It means red heat again, at least at the face, then quenching in a very large tub or creek, then tempering the top to the desired hardness, usually a purple or bronze, with a torch or by suspending upside down over the forge. Alexander Weygers tells how a small homemade anvil can be tempered in his *The Modern Blacksmith.* *

Tricky business. A new plate of carbon steel can be arc-welded over the anvil surface, and not hardened at all. Eighty-point or so carbon which means it contains 0.8 percent carbon—high carbon, will give you a fair surface to work on and usually won't chip.

I have a 300-pound cast anvil that my friend Bill Cameron found for me at $.03 a pound in a Joplin, Missouri, junkyard. It was broken across the corner through the pritchel hole, sloped clear down through the hardened top surface on one side, with a chunk broken out of the top of the horn. I heated it and built up the rounded top corners with an arc-welding rod, using some fifty $\frac{3}{16}$-inch rods. Then I welded a piece of steel into the horn and built up around it with rod. Finally, I ground everything flat and smooth with a sidewinder grinder. At this writing I'm on

* Alexander G. Weygers, *The Modern Blacksmith* (New York: Van Nostrand Reinhold, 1974).

24

the lookout for a 5-inch plate heavy enough to weld on top, through which I'll cut the new hardy and pritchel holes.

That's a lot of work for an anvil, but it's still cheap. And I got a lot of use from it before I started the restoration.

It's best, of course, to find a good anvil and pay the extra money for it. A hundred dollars will usually buy a fair one at auction, or from the rare farmer who'll sell you the old one out in the barn. And considering that you won't wear it out in your lifetime, it's a good investment.

Or you may use a section of railroad rail, cut to a point with an acetylene torch and ground smooth. This is nice steel, and will do quite well for small jobs. I've made several of these, sometimes welding a plate on top, with the hardy and pritchel holes in it, to overhang the tail of the rail anvil.

You'll find the shape of the London anvil, the shape we see most often, handy for your work, which will soon let you see how inconvenient a simple block of iron or a square-cut section of rail would be. Even a worn or chipped anvil will let you do some quite good work. I'll usually use a worn anvil a ridiculously long time before I undertake the replating or milling necessary to put it back in shape.

If you're the type who makes friends with the neighbors easily, you may be able to get on good enough terms with an old farmer up the road to borrow his anvil, particularly if he's not using it, but has too much attachment for it to sell it. It's hard to ruin an anvil, and if you exercise care you won't even dent it with long use. And if you sweeten the deal with free work for the farmer now and then, a loan like this can be parlayed into a sale, eventually, or even a gift.

It is a shame so many anvils were gathered up and sold as junk iron during the fever days of World War II. Our parents or grandparents often patriotically gave away equipment they could not foresee as ever being needed or worth anything again.

The anvil's mass is as important as its shape, so if you fabricate one, make it heavy. A railroad rail anvil is better if you weld slabs of steel on each side of it for more mass. I have shaped small anvils from odd pieces of iron of all kinds, using forge, cutting torch, and arc welder. Whatever you do, the anvil is one of the two pieces of equipment you'll use most in your shop, so keep at it till you have a good one.

The vise is the next heavy tool you'll need, and I've never seen an improvement on the old leg, stump, or box blacksmith's vise. The long leg lets you stabilize it better than any flat-bench mounting for a machinist's vise, and it's meant for light hammering on, as well as holding for bending and twisting.

I have 4-inch, 5-inch, and 6-inch leg vises, only one of which came complete. When searching among the junk for one, see that the screw is good and tight, not worn badly, and that the jaws are in fair

Six-inch blacksmith's leg vise. This one was a gift from Bill Cameron. It was missing the spring and mounting bracket, which I forged.

shape. Everything else is easily repaired. There's a method given in M. T. Richardson's *Practical Blacksmithing*,* a collection of early procedures from individual smiths, for rethreading the screw, but it's not easy.

Most often the opening spring will be gone, and often too, the mounting bracket that also holds the spring. The bar handle that is intact will also be rare. I'm replacing a bar on a family heirloom 6-inch vise, complete with ball at each end, for my friend Muskrat Murphy at this writing. The vise belonged to his wife's grandfather, or I'd try to talk them out of it.

If the jaws are loose so that the movable one flops from side to side like a worn pocketknife blade, all you need do is tighten the joint. A big washer will sometimes do, but you may want to heat the joint in the forge and hammer the joint closed. Remember that the vise is carbon steel, and don't quench it to cool it after heat or it'll be brittle.

The jaws themselves will be worn to some extent, and if badly, you can arc weld bars of medium carbon steel over them. You can also groove the faces of the jaws for better holding, but this will put a pattern in the hot iron you shape in them.

The mounting bracket is a simple piece, with a slot for a tapered wedge to hold the vise tight. Since the fixed jaw upright that the bracket holds is tapered itself, you can shape your bracket smaller, then drive the upright down into it. The return spring goes into this bracket as it comes around the upright, and extends down, to push open the jaws from just above the pivot.

I use leaf spring for the vise return spring, hammered to shape, then quenched and tempered to a blue. See Chapter Five, on tempering, for specifics. Hammer ears on the spring to keep it in place, or it can slip past the movable vise leg, and do you permanent damage as you stand in front of it.

Leg vises are going up in price now, being more and more antique-shop items. I've bought leg vises for as little as $10 recently and seen them as high as $85.

A machinist's vise is a good enough substitute, but will cost more, and doesn't allow the freedom of space for difficult bends, being mounted on a bench. The T-shaped head and jaws of the leg vise let you bend hot steel down into a tight U shape, or form a hoop, or do most other blacksmithing jobs much easier.

You may forge any of several shapes of jaw surfaces for your vise; such surfaces can be slipped over the existing jaws for holding odd shapes. These are handy for ornamental ironwork, where you're doing compound bends and twists.

You'll need hammers of all sorts, but I'll list a few that will get

*M. T. Richardson, *Practical Blacksmithing*, 4 vols. (New York: M. T. Richardson Co., 1890).

A collection of smithing hammers (from left, top): 1½-lb. ball peen; very light cross-peen; 2-lb. ball peen; 3-lb. welding hammer; 3-lb. 45° peen (right-handed); 8-lb. sledge. (bottom) 1-lb. ball peen; 1-lb. cross peen; 6-lb. sledge; 12-oz. ball peen. Hammer heads are put on hot, with the holes expanded, then wedged.

you started. Depending on your brawn, your mainstay will be a straight or cross-peen hammer of 2 to 4 pounds. I use a 3-pound one, hand-forged, but forging hammers is more work that it's worth. Flea markets will yield usable hammer heads for $1.00 or so each, and you'll spend most of half a day forging one.

Add a smaller hammer, about 16 ounces for close work, and a six-to-ten-pound sledge for when you have help. A small ball-peen (12 ounces) will let you rivet and decorate, and a 2-pound one will get bigger jobs of this kind done quicker.

Tongs are limitless in design, being developed for specific kinds of work. Quite often you'll find special tongs no one can tell you the original use of. Some inventive smith probably made them for one of his specialties, which may have been a one-time project or a way of working that died with him.

For close work, like knife blades, I use a tightly closing pair of short-handled, 10-inch tongs my brother made for me from old horsehoof nippers. A longer 18-inch pair is for bigger work, and their flat jaws barely close completely. Another pair the same size has rounded jaws for holding round stock. Yet another 18-inch pair has diamond-shaped jaws for square stock.

A very handy pair has narrow jaws with a rounded notch for holding chain or other small stock to be forge welded. A flat-jawed pair will let the white-hot iron slip before you can hammer it together. Another special pair has one curved, grooved jaw and a short, angle-bent notched one for holding the chain link while you shape it; the pair was designed by my friend, blacksmith Shad Heller. Shaping chain links with flat-jawed tongs is a pain.

And I have dozens of other pairs of tongs, some quite large, that I've collected over the years. One pair is notable: It's a wide-jaw set, with

Hammer or axe-eye tongs. These are handy to hold the head of the tool, through the handle hole. I use them a lot in forging splitting mauls from old sledgehammer heads.

The tongs I use most (from left): chain link welding tongs; large, lengthwise grooved tongs; hammer-eye tongs; flat-jawed, round stock or bolt tongs; short pair with vee-groove for small general work. All these are hand-forged.

29

right-angle bends inward at the jaw tips, for holding hammerheads or axe-heads at the eye for forging. Quite handy.

You'll find special wagon-tire tongs and other pairs that won't do you much good in general work. You can forge any of these yourself from mild steel or medium-carbon steel, unless you have a good source for the tongs cheap. I figure that a pair in good shape that costs under $3.00 is a good buy, because it takes me over an hour to make a pair. Of course, the pair I make will be more tailored to my specific needs, so more valuable to me. My beginning students usually take over half a day to forge a pair; this is about right.

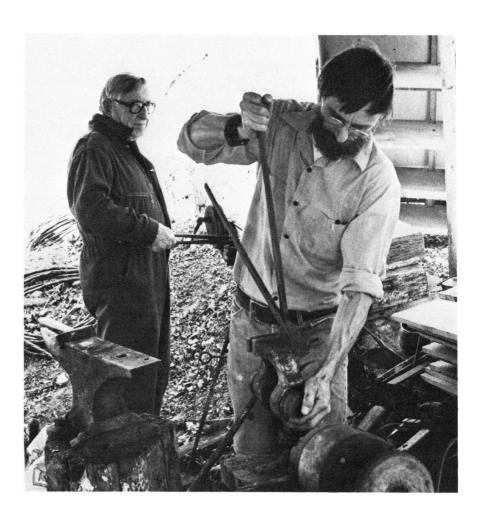

I'm reclaiming a pair of rusted tongs here, while my longtime helper, Bill Cameron, works the portable forge. I've freed the pin, and am here bending the heated jaws for a better fit. Good used tongs are worth buying, since you'll spend half a day or more making your first pair.

Hot cuts, cold chisels, hardies, punches, and drifts all can be forged easily. The hot cut, which is a chisel with a handle, is hardest, because punching the hole for the handle will take time. An old hammerhead is a good piece of steel for this, with the striking face softened so you won't chip off pieces of jagged steel.

The hardy, an anvil-mounted chisel, is easily forged of automotive axle steel, which is medium carbon and quite tough. You don't want this tool hard, because sooner or later you'll miss and take a chunk off it with the hammer.

I recall forging a 30-pound digging bar for Bill Cameron one day. We were cutting 1⅛-inch square stock, with him holding the iron on the hardy and me swinging the short-handled 6-pound sledge. I hit short, glanced off the corner of the hardy, and the hammer flew out of my hands, smashing into my right leg just below the knee. Bill says I chewed up a lot of grass around the shop before I calmed down. If the hardy had been brittle, I'd probably have had shrapnel to deal with, too.

With axle steel of 30-to-50-point carbon, tempering isn't necessary. Just hammer the hardy to shape, fitting it both ways into the hardy hole (which won't be exactly square), then anneal or normalize to sharpen. We talk more about this process in Chapter Five. Heat to cherry red and quench. There isn't enough carbon in the steel to harden it to a brittle stage. If in doubt, do draw the temper to a bronze. You can always reharden if it's too soft.

Punches and chisels include (top, left side): ⅜-inch round punch, standard cold chisel, center punch, ⅛-inch punch. (top, right) Square punch, round drift, long-taper cold chisel for soft metals, awl for punching sheet metal.

Set tools (those struck with a hammer) and others (from top, left side). Square drift, round drift, handled cold chisel, hardy, file. (right) Small flatter, fuller set (the right-hand piece goes into the hardy hole, where the hot metal is laid on it and struck with the other piece to make a stepped-down, even indentation), hot chisel, nail and rivet heading bar.

If you want a cold hardy, one for cutting steel cold like a cold chisel, it must be harder. Use at least 80-point carbon, as in heavy leaf or coil spring steel. Or jackhammer drill steel, which is higher in carbon. Quench and temper draw to a purple. If that's too soft, heat, quench, and draw to bronze. It's better to have a tool too soft than to have it break. Again, I explain all this more in Chapter Five.

If you do a lot of forge work (if, say, you plan to make your living at it), you'll soon wish for a trip-hammer. This is a ponderous mechanical hammer that strikes a series of very rapid, heavy blows on its own anvil. It's foot-operated, so it lets you have both hands to hold things. It's a godsend in forge welding separate pieces, and it will speed production immensely.

I have an ancient one I traded for that originally was powered from an overhead line shaft with flat-belt pulleys—probably steam powered or even water powered. Its last owner was metal sculptor Henry Menke, who'd owned an ornamental iron business before. He powered the trip-hammer with a three-phase electric motor, which I replaced with a single-phase 1½ horsepower model. I have about $200 in it to date, and it's worth every penny.

Bob Patrick, of Bethel, Missouri, bought a later-model trip-hammer at auction for $50, mostly because no one else knew what it was. They're always cumbersome and impossibly hard to move, so you can sometimes get one cheap if it's in the way. They shake any building when they're running. Also, you can get maimed in one.

You can keep acquiring blacksmithing tools and equipment till you have a warehouseful. But add a grinder of some sort to the equipment we've talked about and you're set for most jobs, even without a trip-ham-

Miscellaneous tools include (left side): tinsnips, bullet-mold lead melting ladle used as a forge dipper, forge poker, coal shovel. (right) Hacksaw, adjustable square, steel tape.

David Morris's hand drill press, almost identical to mine. He's modernized it with an added universal chuck. The ratchet feed at top is adjustable, keeps the bit biting the iron.

My trip hammer, not set up for use. The bail, or foot control, partly visible at the bottom allows the smith to use both hands to hold the pieces to be worked. This is an ancient, 1½-horsepower model by Novelty Iron Works, in Iowa.

A handy tool, this shear is made of two lengths of cutting-edge steel, with a square shank for the anvil hardy hole. Iron or steel is cut while red hot, with downward pressure and hammer blows if necessary.

mer. A grinder can be a slick, shielded, double-shaft electric one or an old hand grindstone.

A cheap, powered one is simply an electric motor with an arbor adapter and an abrasive wheel. You can even find a motor free, usually, if the starting mechanism is bad. There's no trick to giving it a spin as you turn it on to start. My lawyer friend Turner White has a manual starter in his blacksmith shop and so do I. Get at least ⅓ horsepower or you'll bog it down.

Beware of secondhand grinding wheels, particularly if you plan to turn them fast. The standard 1,725 revolutions per minute will keep most stones intact, but a geared-up speed can shatter one and kill you, as one did a machinist acquaintance of mine recently. And have a tool bar near the wheel to rest the work on so you won't jam pieces into it.

Handy odd tools are this threading tap (top left), reamer, and threading die. You can make your own bolts and nuts for special projects, or use them for cleaning up battered or rusty threads. The reamer is for enlarging holes cold.

A shear will let you cut hot iron and steel straight and smooth. It's like a large pair of tinsnips with long blades, to be mounted conveniently in the hardy hole of the anvil. Instead of handles, the top blade is operated by hammering down along the stationary bottom one for the cutting action. Or the top blade can have an extended handle from its tip for hand leverage in cutting.

Another unnecessary but handy tool I have is an antique drill press. It has a big snake-spoke flywheel and hand crank, with an automatic ratchet feed. You'll punch most holes hot in your forgework, but there are times when this is awkward, and the drill press is useful. Simpler variations can be had for $10 to $15 at farm sales.

A tap and die set for coarse and fine threads will let you make bolts and nuts for unusual uses a lot cheaper than at hardware-store prices. With the swing to metric sizes, more old sets are becoming available. Try the tools out to make sure the threads are not worn beyond use. One of the handiest uses of a tap and die set is as threadchasers, to clean the threads of rusted or battered bolts or nuts.

A bit of advice here. Learn to use these hardened-steel tools before you break them or wear them out from ignorance. A small tap will snap if forced through a hole dry or too quickly. Alternate forward and backward twists with plenty of cutting oil will keep the tools cool, sharp, and intact. Visit a machine shop and watch the techniques.

Finally, you'll want to house your workshop effectively, but cheaply. I've just built one in the woods at our new place, a 12-by-16-foot shed-roofed, open-sided version of the pole barn. It will later be enclosed for winter work, with double doors for getting at least the ends of vehicles to work on in out of the rain. It began with just four timber uprights, set on flat stones on the ground. A post hole next to each timber was filled with concrete, into which went a heavy metal bar, bolted to the upright, with a cross pin down in the concrete.

That keeps the structure stable, without letting the timbers rot (as they would set into either the ground or the concrete; water would run down into the crack between the concrete and wood and rot the wood). Overhead these uprights are notched and pinned to sloping stringers (end timbers overhead) that overhang front and back. Purlins, which function as rafters, are pinned to these, and galvanized roofing is laid on the purlins. The whole thing is angle-braced.

The shop took two days to build, but that included hewing the timbers and working the notched joints. It could have been spiked up in a day, of round poles. The roof cost $70, which could have been nearer $50 if I'd been able to get in on a special sale of corrugated roofing. The other materials were growing on the place or in my scrap pile. One wheelbarrowload of mixed concrete filled the four holes, which I widened at the bottom to give more stability.

The commercial shop I built in Hollister, Missouri, is also small, 12 by 16 feet again, but is framed of 8-by-8-inch timbers, with a peaked, shingled roof. It has a 3-foot stone wall around it, with an opening for a wrought-iron gate. Part of the wall is the masonry forge, which is built in. This shop is more elaborate, and was built to allow visitors to watch the work inside. It also conforms to the stone-and-half-timber building style of the English-looking town.

In spite of this smithy's small size, I've taught several courses there, with as many as half a dozen students working. Unless you have a lot of equipment or need space to store long lengths of steel, a small shop is adequate.

For a floor I use raked gravel, which is easier on feet than concrete. Security's no problem at home, but I lock up small tools at the village shop, and have blower, anvil, and vise bolted down and spotwelded to slow their removal.

Do get your operation under a roof of some kind. The spreading chestnut trees are all gone now, with the turn-of-the-century blight, and wouldn't give your smithy much protection anyway. Rain water can get into your blower, freeze and burst it overnight, and things like files are ruined by rust.

I've heard of smiths using teepees, vans, and trailers for shops; yours, of course, is a matter of your own inclination. I know of several in the limerock country that are simply back under overhanging bluff ledges—shallow caves.

You'll develop a sense of pride in forgework well done, and this can extend to your smithy. I like wrought-iron decorative work in evidence, and construction strengthened with examples of my smithing. This is more important if you plan to make part or all of your living from your shop. Blacksmith shops are usually dirty, dark, and full of what is, to the nonsmith, junk. A relatively neat shop adorned with some of your best work will encourage commissions.

A simple touch I use is my slack tub, which is half a 60-gallon oak whiskey barrel. It's no more efficient than a galvanized tub or large bucket, but I get lots of comments on it. Similarly, I have my anvils spiked in place on their blocks with fitted forged staples, with hooks and loops for tools. Aside from the convenience, this arrangement makes people think I actually know how to use all those fascinating tools.

CHAPTER THREE

Coal, Iron, and Steel

Keeping a supply of materials will constitute most of your smithy overhead, after you've put the basic shop together. And of the three materials, good coal will be hardest to find.

Blacksmith coal is simply a low-sulfur, good-coking coal, usually soft coal, in pebble-size chunks. It should last a long time, and produce few, if any, clinkers. The difficulty today is that the low demand makes it unprofitable for coal companies to keep their product clean and of the high quality demanded for forgework. Just about any coal will burn in a heating furnace or power plant, the EPA permitting. (I hope the EPA can keep us breathing longer.) So why bother with top quality for a very small blacksmithing market?

You can use furnace coal in your forgework. It'll get the iron hot, all right, but the sulfur fumes will lift off the top of your head, the smoke will endear you to none of even your distant rural neighbors, and you'll have a mass of clinkers in the forge very soon. Forget forge welding altogether with this coal. A clinker's crude metallic substance melted out of the coal gives off oxides, making it impossible to do good welding.

I launched a commercial shop once, in a region that had no good coal supply, using furnace coal spilled along the railroad tracks. Seems the nearby college power-plant coal was loaded into trucks periodically, and the drivers hotrodded across a shallow stream as they started off. Spilled coal was almost a foot deep along the road, crushed fine by the truck tires. The coal smoked, smelled, and made my eyes smart, but I did a lot of work with it. It did burn up fast, but the price was so right.

Now, the question I'm asked most frequently by other smiths is the location of my coal source. It's been bad and it's been good.

I used a one-man coal company in Oklahoma for a while. He dug coal till he had a truckload, then came East, supplying his few but faithful shops with 100-pound sackfuls as he went. The proceeds went for really bad whiskey, and there was a regular cycle of booze up, sober up, dig up,

This clinker is made up of crude metallic substances melted out of the coal. Oxides given off by it will keep you from making a forge weld, and the clinker itself will clog up the air passage (tuyere) in the forge. Clinkers appear in the bottom of the fire as dark objects.

(opposite)
The forge fire will burn high and smoky until it converts the raw coal to coke. Keep pulling coal up to the fire as you turn the blower, and keep a good flame to burn off the smoke. Finally, wet down the raw coal and pack it into a cave-like shape, with clean-burning coke inside. Then it's ready for the iron.

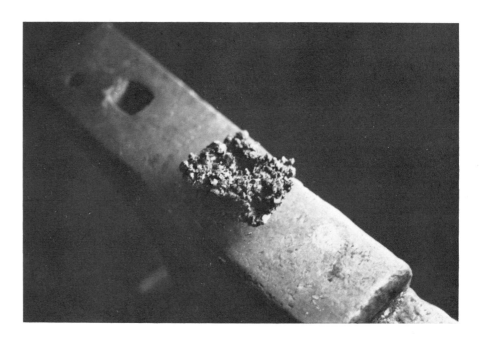

and load up, between supply runs. But the coal was good, until he got to loading up with surface stuff around other mines to save the work of digging: I had to stop using his coal, and so did most of the other smiths in the region.

I'd heard again and again of a lumber company in a distant town that had good coal, and I even used some of it a friend had. I finally made the 300-mile round trip for a load, only to discover that their supplier had just gone out of business, and they had another brand I'd already tried and rejected.

Really distant suppliers in industrial centers could and did ship good coal but I actually paid more for the freight than for the coal. Finally, Bill Cameron located a mine supply company in Joplin, Missouri, that had good coal cheap, and it was close enough for a trip now and then.

The composition of the coal—anthracite or bituminous or whatever—isn't as important as its coking qualities and whether it burns clean and lasts. You see, the fire, along with sprinkled water, steams and burns out the tar and sulfur and converts the fuel to coke, which is very high in carbon and burns clear. Only the coke should come in contact with the iron you're forging. As it burns out, you bring in more, keeping raw coal away from the center of the fire.

The best path to good coal is still asking other smiths. If none are around, or if they're having the same problem, try the offerings of the coal companies in the area. If this doesn't work, widen your search area. It takes only a sample bucketful of coal to see how it will burn, and trying it out is a necessity.

Coke can be bought outright, but is expensive and usually not available in small quantities. I never buy more than a ton of coal at a time, and usually split that much several ways among other smiths. That's a fair pickup truckload.

Charcoal was the backwoods blacksmith's mainstay. He made his own by keeping air away from burning oak, hickory, or maple logs once the fire was going well. You can do this too, or try to find log charcoal for sale. The briquets are pulverized charcoal that's mixed with a binder like cornstarch, to allow for sales-oriented shaping. That reduces carbon content, which should be as high as possible.

I've made charcoal simply by lifting hot coals from the fireplace and dropping them into a bucket of water. You can build a log fire in a pit, then cover it with sheet iron and plaster up the cracks with clay. The fire will burn very slowly with so little oxygen, finally going out, leaving some good charcoal, some ashes, and some wood. With practice you'll learn how big a fire, when to cover it, and what to expect.

Charcoal makes a very clean forge fire, good for welding. Charcoal's big shortcoming is that it burns up fast. Good coal will last many times longer. Even bad coal has more energy in it than charcoal.

A gas forge is also clean, and can be built with firebrick, piped gas, and a blower. You don't get enough heat for welding, but this also means you can leave steel in the forge without burning up the steel. Also, the gas forge, which is sort of a contained-flame blowtorch, heats a larger area, so you can have a dozen irons in the fire at once. Good for production work. But the price of liquid petroleum gas is climbing (hurtling?) and that's about all you'll be able to get in the backwoods. Natural gas will do well if you are on a line.

We should also mention use of the oxygen and acetylene torch to heat your metal. This is done by some smiths at crafts fairs and indoor exhibits, but it's expensive. The torch is good for temper drawing, however, which we'll discuss later.

Iron and steel are your raw materials, besides fuel. For simplicity, I'll call mild steel, iron; carbon or tool steel will be just steel here. I recycle for most of my metal, but sometimes I must buy stock. I keep a supply of rods ¼-inch, ⅜-inch, and ½-inch square and round, some bar stock from ⅛-inch up to ½-inch thick, from ½-inch to 2½ inches wide. Odd sizes of angle iron are also useful.

For the special order, I'll often buy an unusual dimension of iron. Digging bars are usually 1½ inches round or square, 5 to 6 feet long. A

Wayne Haymes shows me the gas forge he built of firebrick. He used a squirrel-cage blower with adjustable draft, feeding air through flexible exhaust pipe. His gas pipe with cut-off valve had no orifice or nozzle, but was brazed into the side of the two-inch steel pipe air inlet. He was able to do production smithing with 8 to 10 irons in the fire with this forge.

broadaxe usually requires ¼-inch plate. I sometimes buy new steel for knives.

This steel is available from the steelyard, which will be located in any sizable town. There are cutting and delivery charges, but lengths are often 20 feet, awkward unless you have a vehicle equipped for moving such lengths. A pickup truck can carry an over-the-cab rack—easily built—which is also handy for long boards, poles, and sections of pipe.

By far most of my iron and steel is recycled, and comes from the most commonplace sources, and the most unlikely as well. Automotive coil and leaf springs are mainstays for high-carbon steel, and are good for knives, chisels, axes, punches, machetes, prybars, and, of course, other springs.

A coil spring of eight loops 4 inches in diameter yields over 8 feet of steel bar. A used garage-door spring gave me over 50 feet of ¼-inch rod, which over the years has become woodcarvers' knife blades, small punches, pivot pins in tongs and shears, nails, and screwdrivers. This spring cost $.50. The heavier car springs may be from $.25 to $1.00 if they're lying out in the junkyard, orphaned, and rusting. If they're attached to an identifiable vehicle, they're considered replacement parts and cost more.

Leaf springs are so very handy, except they're often too wide. A cutting torch or a stationary shear to fit into the anvil hardy hole will cut them to size. I use them full width for froes, cutting across at the tie-bolt to get stock for two from one leaf. Drawknives require only about 1 inch of width, so I use the shear to split the springs.

Old hayrake teeth are good steel, too. You can tell a lot about the steel you find if you know what it's been used for before. Hayrake teeth are about the same high carbon content as springs, 80 to 100 points. Axle steel is 30 to 50 points, or medium. Woodsaw blades are medium, too, which is tough steel rather than hard steel. Reinforcing rod production is not carefully controlled, often using recycled steel from whatever is on the yard at the time. Rebar is usually about like axle steel, temperable, but not high enough in carbon content for chisels, punches, or rock tools, and not really predictable enough.

Good steel is often the wrong size. Axle steel is a good example. One of my students wanted a Bowie knife from a 1½-inch axle, and we took turns helping him hammer it. It was a little soft for a knife, but he'd broken knives throwing them, and this steel is by its nature almost a guarantee against that.

When buying steel, you may run into numerical classifications, such as 4140, 3130. The thing to remember is that the last two figures denote carbon content in points. This is not true of all steels, however.

The average old-time smith had little knowledge of steel's carbon content as it related to hardening and tempering, as we said in Chapter

Blacksmithing iron and steel are to be had free, as junk everywhere. The long piece here was an automotive helper spring that became a froe and two drawknives. The piece under it at the other end became one of the set of andirons shown in Chapter Eight.

Bar stock shown here is available by the pound from any steelyard. It usually comes in 20-foot lengths, with cutting extra. Coil springs are often free when not identifiable at the junkyard. They can be heated and straightened (right) in the vise or hammered over the anvil.

JUNKYARD STEEL: Its Approximate Carbon Contents

MILD STEEL	MEDIUM CARBON	HIGH CARBON	TOOL STEEL
Most scrap: bars, rods, angle iron. Chain, some nails,* some bolts.*	Most shafting, tie rods, drive shafts, reinforcing rod (not dependable), frame steel, crankshafts, piston rods, some engine valves† (many are alloys). Pump sucker rod, some bolts, cable, some nails, railroad spikes, many hooks, most saws: circle, crosscut.	Coil and leaf springs, wrenches, torsion bars, some engine valves, hayrake teeth, picks, mattocks, railroad rail, axes.	Grader blade, plow points, drill steel, machine tools, files, rasps, stone working tools.

*Nails, spikes, horseshoes and most bolts are low carbon, somewhere between mild and medium.
†Caution: Avoid sodium-filled engine valves — they are highly dangerous under heat or impact.

In addition, cast iron is not malleable. It is good for heat resistance: it is used in engine blocks, stoves, and cooking pots. Also called gray iron; but is not to be confused with cast steel, which is usually high carbon.

One, and he developed techniques that would have to be called crude today. Also, his supply of steel was erratic and it was not uniform, so he had another handicap. The old accounts say without reservation to temper-draw an axe, for instance, to a blue, which is about right for 80-point steel. But the old handmade axe might be 50-point steel, or 100-point steel, or even wrought iron that is case hardened only on the surface. The old smiths used what they could get, and if they could get enough of the same stuff, they experimented until they could work it reliably.

In the chapter on tempering steels we talk more about choosing the right steel for the right tool, but you'll need to know something before you scrounge a supply. For instance, there's little point in paying a high price for axle steel, generally too thick for most jobs and too short for others, when you already have a pile of small shafting of the same carbon on hand that you got free.

Just because a steel is temperable doesn't make it good for everything. I wouldn't make stone-cutting tools of 30-point axle steel, because it just won't harden enough. Nor would I use an old file of well over 100-

point carbon for a knife or something that has to bend often. The craft center blacksmith's trick of welding steel cable together to make a knife is impressive (and a neat trick), but it makes a low-medium carbon blade that is too soft for most people's tastes.

For more mundane uses, carbon-steel coil spring makes a triangle dinner gong with a clearer, sharper tone than mild steel. It also makes a tougher fireplace poker, but don't quench it to cool it or it'll shatter in use. This steel also makes a dandy pinch bar or cold chisel. Alexander Weygers shows how to unwind coil springs in his *Modern Blacksmith.* I use the vise or hammer and anvil to straighten short sections of heavy springs at a time, but you can unwind light ones from a spindle when hot.

You can find lightweight angle iron in old bedspring sets, along with some small medium-to-high carbon rod. Old shafting is generally medium carbon, about like axle steel. Plow points are higher carbon, as is grader blade, jackhammer stem, and other steel designed for wear against stones and the earth. Old tie rods and drive shafts are about medium carbon.

If the original application didn't require high-carbon steel, it was a waste for the manufacturer to supply it, so use your knowledge of mechanical stresses to guess about a piece that you haven't worked with. Working it is, of course, the best test. Make something out of it and see how it performs, using the principle of drawing to a soft temper first to keep it from breaking; then go up from there.

I honestly don't know a quick way to test for carbon content in a strange piece of steel. You can, it is true, see more sparks that act differently when thrown from a grinder with higher-carbon steel. You can also quench from cherry red and try a file on it. Neither method will tell you much. The quenched-steel method will tell you more if you draw temper to various colors and try the file at each. See Chapter Five for specifics on temper drawing.

Jack Andrews, in his *Edge of the Anvil,** has a brief but handy chart giving the carbon content of commonly found recycled steel items. He and several other published smiths also suggest uses for certain steels, all of which my own experience does not agree with. But I hasten to state that one smith's methods with a given steel will produce results different from those of another. And hardness preference for, say, a knife blade is almost purely a matter of individuality.

Rare metals like Damascus steel and wrought iron are hard to acquire now. Damascus always was, and its fabrication is among the highest forms of the smith's craft. You won't find it in a junkyard. Its layers of very high carbon steel or cast iron alternate with wrought iron, welded together, doubled, welded, often two-hundred times or more. The leg-

---

*Jack Andrews, *Edge of the Anvil* (Emmaus, Pa.: Rodale Press, 1977).

endary swords of Damascus were made this way as a method of getting carbon into wrought iron when this was a major problem.

Wrought iron was the stock-in-trade of the early smith. It welded easily, worked easily, turned a satisfying black with age, and didn't rust badly. Old pieces of it show a pronounced grain instead of the crystalline structure of even mild steel.

In an age of machines, mild steel became preferable to wrought iron, and except for some hand-muddled iron from California and perhaps some still found in Norway and Sweden, I know of none to be had new. Old pieces can be found in very old wagon tires, andirons, hinges—anything forged long enough ago, before the blast furnaces made uniform mild steel so cheap and available.

The late Alex Bealer, pretty much the dean of modern American blacksmiths, discusses the evolution of iron and steel at length in his *The Art of Blacksmithing.** It helps to know the nature of the materials you're working with.

You will certainly acquire a scrap pile of odds and ends around your shop that will contain valuable old iron and steel, no matter what your wife's opinion of it. But resist the urge to scavenge just for the sake of getting it free. If it's doubtful that you'll be able to use a supply of particularly grotesque-shaped iron, leave it for the next fellow. He may think in different twists from yours.

Understand, of course, that iron may be shaped and reshaped countless times, recycled on and on. Steel may lose its temper in a fire, but it can be rehardened and tempered again, unless burned out. You will occasionally run into a piece of old, pitted iron that splits or crumbles when you try to forge it. It's called "red short," and I know of no way to use it, but most old stuff is as good as new.

We mentioned salvage yards. Garages, old barns, demolition sites of all kinds, flea markets, and your neighbor's workshop all are good sources for mild steel, or carbon steel. Most machine shops and equipment maintenance shops have a scrap pile out the back door, and the owner will often part with bits and pieces.

I found a steel bar 1 inch by ½ inch and about 4 feet long many years ago while poking around the burned remains of a late nineteenth-century artist's studio back in the woods. I have no idea what it was used for originally, but I forged a set of chisels and punches from it; these continue to be my basic tools, in spite of a plethora of others acquired and made since.

You will be able to find steel much easier than you can hammer it. And for most jobs you won't have to shell out for new stock, after your own supply dump has grown.

---

*Alex W. Bealer, *The Art of Blacksmithing* (New York: Funk & Wagnalls Co., 1969).

CHAPTER FOUR

Hammering Iron

I have heard several veteran blacksmiths reply to the question of what exactly they do, in this way:

"Well, you get a piece of iron hot, then you hit it with a hammer." And that's what it's all about. Iron and steel are malleable when red hot, and hammering lets the smith shape them by degrees to his purposes. We'll simplify things by referring to mild steel as iron, and carbon steel or tool steel as steel. Sometimes this gets confusing, but you need to know the difference. More than once I've shaped a piece of what I thought was mild steel, then tossed it into the slack tub to cool it, only to have it shatter in use: carbon steel in disguise. It's usually easy to tell that carbon steel is tougher when you're hammering it, but sometimes it gets past you.

The first step is the fire in the forge. First of all, make sure the ashes are dumped and the air passage into the firepot (the tuyere) is clear. Now crumple four pages of newspaper into a tight ball (you'll reduce this to two pages or even one page, later) and lay it or some wood shavings in the bottom of the forge, with coal and coke, if any, raked away to all sides. Light the tinder and, if newspaper, turn it so the flame is at the bottom. Now crank the blower or operate the bellows gently at first, as you rake in a layer of coke from the last fire, and fine coal. Increase the air blast so you don't smother the flames, then add more coke and coal. Now really get on the blower crank and pile coal, coke, or both on top, building a mound at least 6 inches high. This will effectively smother the fire and you'll get a dense smoke, mostly from the newspaper. Poke an air hole down through the center, which will be burning out by now, and you'll get a flame to come up, burning some of that choking smoke off.

Use the poker to push in the sides of the hollow where the newspaper burned out, and repunch the air hole. Now rake coal up from all sides to form a miniature Vesuvius and pack it down with the back of the coal shovel. Keep cranking. You'll see the smoke diminish as the coal turns to coke and the fire clears. When it's out to about a 3-inch diameter,

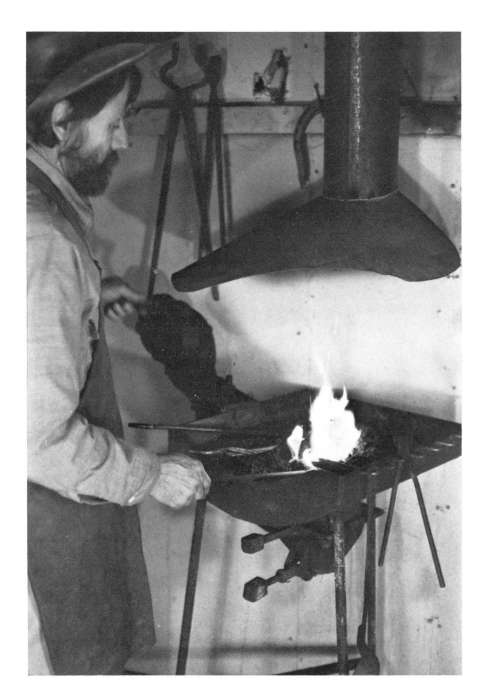

I built this forge around the cast firepot shown underneath. It has a triangular clinker breaker/tuyere, the handle of which I later bent downward to hold the proper alignment, and a trapdoor ash dump, held shut by another weight. The blower was separate, connected here with flexible exhaust pipe.

50

sprinkle water around the edges of it to contain it, and to help steam impurities out of the coal. Use water from time to time to keep the fire where you want it. A tin can with a long handle is handy, maybe with holes punched in the bottom for a sprinkler. I use an old bullet-mold, lead-melting ladle.

Don't put iron into the fire until it clears. Raw coal should not come into contact with the iron, or you'll get melted coal tar all over it, and you won't be able to see what's going on through the smoke. To heat a long section of bar, for instance, let the fire spread out, keeping it narrow with water. And move the bar back and forth to distribute the heat.

With air blasting up from the bottom, the heated iron tends to oxidize faster near the bottom of the fire, and less at the top, where it also absorbs some carbon from the burning coke. It's best to keep the iron down in the fire instead of on top of it, to help hold the heat in. Your fire should be deep, a minimum of the 6 inches we mentioned, and the iron can be 1 inch or 2 inches down. As you heat iron, the core of the fire will keep burning out, so push it in from all sides and bank new coal around the outside, sprinkling a little water each time.

When you leave the fire for a few minutes, heap raw coal over it to make coke while you're gone. The fire will eventually go out, but it'll burn a lot of coal before it does. Drown it when you're through with it to save coal. If you want to keep it going while you do something else, a favorite practice among smiths is to shove a pine knot down into it.

About watering: Don't use too much water, or you'll put out the fire, first of all. And the water will combine with sulfur, burning out of the coal to produce sulfuric acid, which will eat away at the bottom of your forge. That in itself is a good reason not to leave the forge out in the rain, too, a tacky habit at best.

Now let's start with drawing out a piece of iron, a basic step in blacksmithing. Push the end of a ⅜-inch round rod 20 inches long through the lip of the coal mound into the fire. Turn your blower steadily, but not fast for this rod, or you'll just waste coal. As you gain proficiency, you'll have two or more irons in the fire at once for higher production.

Watch the iron through the hole it made when you pushed it into the fire, or pull it out and inspect it. When it's red to about 3 inches from the end, pull it out and stop cranking. The tip may be white hot by now, and always remove the iron before it starts to spark. The sparks are burning iron, and much of this will pit the rod. Any sparks at all will ruin carbon steel, since the fire eats its way down through it.

Dark red heat is the first color you'll notice. You can work mild steel at this temperature, but you won't get much done. Cherry red is a bright glow that will sometimes flicker as you look at it. This is the heat that's usually best for hardening steel, and any iron can be worked here.

When iron starts to give off white sparks, it's burning, and is too hot for anything, even forge welding, contrary to popular belief. Burned iron will pit and be weakened; burned carbon steel will crumble apart when hammered.

IRON/STEEL: Work Chart at Heat Colors

HEAT	FORGING
Dark red	Malleable with some difficulty. Can work iron, but will require harder hammering. Carbon steel will surfacecrack at this heat.
Cherry red	More malleable. Can work iron, low-carbon steels. Quench most steels here for hardness.
Orange	Universally malleable. Can work iron, all steels, punch holes, upset.
Yellow	Easily malleable. Watch for burning. Can work iron, all steels, upset. Welding possible. When working carbon steels, cold hammer lightly while cooling to pack crystalline structure.
White or yellow-white	Welding heat—molten on surface. Watch for burning, particularly if steel or iron is deep down in fire. Cold hammer carbon steels lightly while cooling.

Orange or yellow is hotter, and the iron is more malleable still. Light yellow, which we call white hot, is just before the iron burns. You'll see it glisten, as the surface is actually molten at this heat.

Of course, the hotter the iron, the more you'll be able to do with it before it cools, within limits. It's a good idea to heat the iron back farther than you plan to work it so the cold iron won't draw heat from the hot part. Also, the cold anvil will cool the iron as soon as you lay it on it, so work fast. Of course, the term "striking while the iron is hot" comes from the smithy, along with "losing your temper" and "too many irons in the fire."

Scale, which is oxidation, or instant rust, will form on the iron with each heat. Hot scale will burn you, but won't hurt the metal, unless you heat enough times to take several thousand layers off. Try to keep the number of heats down, especially on carbon steel, because you get pitting as well as scaling.

You may stand anywhere in relation to the anvil you choose, contrary to many an old-timer's belief. It isn't a good idea to impale yourself on the horn as you swing around from the forge, however. Position the anvil block so it's close to the fire but not in the way. It's generally better to crank the blower with your left hand if you're right-handed, which means letting go of the blower to grab iron or tongs as you pick up the hammer in your right hand. If you're left-handed, reverse this.

The anvil should be at knuckle height when standing, for most work. I keep a second one 4 inches higher for light, close work so I don't have to bend over so much.

All right: I've left you holding that red-hot rod for too long. Get it across the anvil face with the tip quite near the far edge. To draw the iron, hit it with the hammer at a slight angle, flattening the iron and pointing it a bit. Turn the iron up on its edge while it's fairly thick to work this side, forming a square, tapering toward a point. If you flatten too much at first, it'll fold when up on edge. Keep moving the tip back from the edge of the anvil as you hammer, which will lengthen, or draw, it.

Turn often, which will keep the square shape, still somewhat pointed. Now, if you're reducing the rod to a given size, draw the tip to that size first, then direct your hammering to the thicker part of the rod to match the end. If you're pointing, as for a nail, a hook, or a tapered loop, take the tip all the way to a point. Let the face of the hammer hang over the edge of the anvil a bit, so you won't knock dents in the anvil face. Use a lighter blow on the tip, and reheat as the red fades. Steel will often split if you hammer it thin too cold. Once pointed, watch closely in the fire; it will burn easily.

Drawing iron to a point. The flat hammer face and the flat anvil give you flat surfaces, of course, so when turned up on edge and hammered, you get a square when drawing iron. It can be rounded again by standing on the corners, hammering to an octagon, then rolling and hammering round.

About hammering: Use an elbow action, holding the handle as far toward the end as is comfortable. You'll hear admonitions to hold it only by the extreme end from other smiths, carpenters, and assorted busybodies. Hold it where it feels right and gets the job done. Period. But do rest the hammer on the anvil every few strokes.

I'm reminded of my friend tinsmith T. A. Hart, who was working in another man's shop some years ago, learning the trade.

"Quit choking that hammer!" the old tinner yelled at him. T.A. explained that he had better control up close the way he was doing it. The old man was unimpressed.

"In this shop you'll learn to hammer right!" he roared.

Now, T.A. has a stubborn streak, so he determined to hammer whatever way felt best, which happened to be with his hand about halfway up the handle. Finally, the old smith could stand it no longer. He grabbed the hammer from his apprentice and ran the handle through a nearby table saw, cutting off the part that wasn't getting used.

"Now at least we won't waste that extra wood," he said. T.A. took the hammer back and went to work again, quietly: This was not the reaction the old man expected from his hotheaded apprentice. T.A. hammered on.

"Didn't it bother you for me to saw your hammer in two?"

"Hell, no. That's your hammer. Cut 'em all off if you want to, you crazy old man." Still hammering.

I've put in a lot of hammer strokes, and except for the wise-mouthed old codger at every crafts fair, nobody tells me how to hold a hammer. That old man is unavoidable. I sometimes hand him the hammer without a word, or offer to bet him I can hit his finger if laid on the anvil, even though I'm not holding the hammer right.

Generally, heavy blows can be directed with more accuracy from the end of the handle, light ones from farther up. And accuracy is important. I was once shaping a Bowie knife blade on the anvil at a crafts fair, slamming away with a ball-peen hammer, bending close. I missed clean, and the hardened hammer came up off the hardened anvil like a shot, scoring one on me right between the eyes. The crowd loved it, probably thinking the blood running down my nose was all part of an act. Wanted me to do it again for them.

You will wear yourself out pecking lightly at heavy steel all day when you could whop it harder faster, but with a selection of hammers from 16 ounces or less up to 4 to 6 pounds, you can get the feel of hitting the iron effectively. The object is to shape the iron, and try to retain the function of your arm in the process.

Heeling the hammer is holding the handle too low, so the face is not parallel to the anvil face. Toeing it is the opposite. Proper anvil height and a proper swing, which has some push from the shoulder in it, will get the hammer down flat.

Back to our piece of iron. This squaring is the first step, because the hammer and anvil are flat, and anything you hammer is going to flatten. If you want it round again, turn the squared rod up on its corners and hammer it eight-sided. Now roll it and tap it round. Keep hammering until it's as smooth as you want it. Old-time smiths wanted machinelike smoothness to their work, but you'll find yours is appreciated more if the hammer marks show. Why would anyone pay for hand work if it looks machine made? But don't get sloppy. There's a broad range of workmanship between slick factory-precision and botchery.

I start students on nail making, that old apprentice beginning job that went on and on before machine-cut square nails almost two hundred years ago. Nail making was often a cottage industry, and folks hammered nails by the fireside in winter or at small forges set up at home.

The rod is drawn to a point, left square, and inserted through a tapered hole in a tool called the nail bar. If the right length sticks through as it tightens up in the taper, mark a spot about ⅜ inch past the big end at

Cutting off iron on the hardy. The piece is cut from both sides for a more even end.

The final blow in cutting should be just alongside the hardy, to shear off the iron. This piece is a carbon-steel tooth for a rock rake.

55

the bar, on the hardy. If the nail's too short, hammer it some more. Now take the rod out of the bar, heat again, and cut it from at least two opposite sides on the hardy, almost through. Stick the rod back into the nail bar and break off the rod at the cut. Now push the rod back into the fire, put the nail point-down into the pritchel hole in the anvil, and rivet a head onto the nail. Quickly.

If you cut the nail from one side only on the hardy, the iron will lean over as you head it, and the head will all be to one side, like a railroad spike. Some of the ⅜ inch you left for the head will jam down into the bar, but you should have enough left. Rivet with either the flat hammer, or the ball peen for a decorative effect. Now quench bar and all in the slack tub, which will contract the hot nail and let it out of the bar.

That's how nails were made for thousands of years. Today handforged nails are chiefly decorative. I pin pot hooks to beams with them, or hang my tools on them, or do a quick demonstration at a fair. Once I get going I can do a nail in one heat, but there's a trick to it. The trick is placing the cut-off rod back in the fire as you head the nail, so there's still enough heat in it to draw the next nail without another heat.

Bending hot iron is done best by hanging it over the edge or the horn of the anvil and hammering the iron downward; or setting the end on the anvil, holding the other end out, and hitting it in the middle; or clamping it in the vise and bending it. Let's say you want to make that tapered point into a hook instead of a nail. Lay it across the horn near the point, hot, with about ¼ inch over, and hammer the end down. Move more rod out at each blow, and the tip will curve down and under.

Now lay the hook on its back on the anvil face and tap the tip down to where you want it. If the bend is irregular, slip it over the point of the horn and round it up. If you want a reverse bend at the shank of the hook like a question mark, hang it, back upward, on the horn and hit it downward at the shank. If you want the tip of the hook to curve outward, hang just this tip on the horn, back downward, and hit it about ¼ inch back from the tip.

Shaping iron is all logic. You have to hit the iron for a while to see how each blow will affect it, but before long you'll be able to get some economy into your hammering. Heat as often as necessary. You should be able to draw a 3-inch-square point on ⅜-inch rod in one heat with some practice. I'm not as fast as some smiths, but I routinely draw and point a 2-inch hook, bend it, and mark it on the hardy for cutoff in one heat. Use a big hammer to get the job done faster.

I'll say here that most beginners are afraid of hitting the iron too hard. Remember that you can reshape any mistake you're liable to make from hitting too hard, so go ahead and slam it. There's a lot to be said for getting the basic shaping done with a big hammer while it's hot. You can finish with lighter blows later.

(top left)
One method of forming a loop handle. The stock is drawn to a point, then rounded.

(top right)
Then the point curved over the horn.

(center left)
The point is brought on around from below.

(center right)
The piece is laid on its back to close the loop.

(bottom left)
The reverse curve is hammered into the shank. An alternate method is to bend here at a right angle first, then form the loop in the bent part.

(bottom right)
If a reversed tip is desired, it's put in last, then the loop trued up.

Turner White, as a student in one of my courses, upsets the end of a poker to form an ornamental ball. A Springfield, Missouri, attorney, he has a forge at his farm.

Turner White puts a decorative twist into a fireplace poker. The point is the forge-welded bird's-beak design.

For a loop, as in the end of a poker, heat a longer section of the rod. For precision, mark the beginning of the loop first, with soapstone or a nick with a file or chisel, and bend a right angle on the edge of the anvil. Now turn the rod over, and start the bend as you did with the hook, over the anvil horn. With luck the tip will curl under and finally touch at the first bend. Adjust the circle on the horn. You may want to cool just the right-angle bend a bit in the tub before you start the loop, to keep from straightening it too much, but it'll usually be near the cold iron and this won't be necessary.

Usually I don't make a loop this way. I start the loop with the point, finish it to size, then hang it on the horn and put the reverse bend in last to get the loop centered. Both these methods give you a functional, plain loop.

Now try drawing another rod to a taper, rounding it, then looping, keeping the pointed tip bent outward. Makes a nice piece of work. A variation is to hammer the tip flat but not pointed, round the corners, and make a reverse bend at the end of the loop. You will develop your own preferences. In time, who knows? Collectors will be able to identify your work by its distinctive touches.

Twisting is a decorative operation applied to square stock, or squared sections of round, or bundles of rods. Heat the entire part to be twisted by moving the rod back and forth in the fire to an even red. Now clamp in the vise and twist with tongs, locking pliers, or if you have a loop in the end, with a bar through. A light twist produces a spiral, more gives a tighter look.

Twisting is also a corrective measure if your fireplace poker, say, doesn't come out with its offset point parallel to the loop in the handle. Often a piece will need a twist to get it aligned after it's finished.

Upsetting is a more complicated operation, which thickens the iron instead of thinning it. The metal is heated, then jammed from the end to spread it. A ball on the end of a rod is a common upsetting operation. Heat the end, then hammer from this or the other end against the anvil. Watch the edges that will mushroom out, and keep them hammered in. Once the thin edge folds over, it must either be ground off or welded on again. And welding will thin the upset. Repeat the heating and hammering until you have a mass of metal to shape into the ball.

This is a frustrating process for beginners. Very little progress is made with each heat, since keeping the edges hammered in tends to reverse the upsetting process. Most smiths prefer to hammer a ball from larger stock, punch it, and then weld or rivet the bar into it.

I learned another method of upsetting from Bob Patrick; this is to bend the end of the rod at a right angle, then lay the rod on its back on the face of the anvil and upset the bent end back into the main rod. Take care here not to let the bend become a fold. This bend/upset can be repeated as often as necessary.

Some smiths upset the ends of rods to be welded so there'll be extra metal to compensate for the thinning by hammering the weld. I don't do this, since there are two thicknesses in the lapped joint anyway.

To make a simple right-angle bend, hang the iron over the edge of the anvil, hammering down and then inward to the side of the anvil, and on top again. The iron will stretch at the outside of the bend and be rounded here. If you need a sharp right angle at the outside of the bend too, you'll need to upset as you bend.

To do this, make the basic bend, then heat and shape a loop of the angle on the horn. Now place this shape back on the edge of the anvil, and hammer outward toward the bend from each side. That pushes metal toward the bend, upsetting there. Finally, shape the right angle again in the extra iron you've upset. This makes a stronger bend, since there's more metal there.

The basic technique of drawing hot iron can be speeded up by using the peen of the hammer first to create a series of humps, which are later hammered flat. The hammer shown here has a 45-degree peen instead of the standard straight or cross peen.

When you hammer iron, you stretch it. This is important to know for several reasons. If you plan to hammer a round or square rod into a flat piece for, say, a knife blade, your 8-inch rod may be a foot long when you're through. The narrow hammer peen can be used to direct the stretching better. Used parallel to the rod, the peen will flatten it without lengthening it so much. Used the other way it will stretch it more.

To draw any iron more quickly, use the peen across the rod, skipping spaces, to make humps. Then hammer the humps out with the face of the hammer. Once flat, you'll bend your knife blade up when you taper it to the edge. Again the peen, used along the length, will reduce this bending. I have no doubt that the curve of knife edges is the natural shape from tapering during forging. It also makes it more efficient for slicing.

Another method for offsetting the bend when a knife blade is tapered is to bend the basic steel bar the other way before beginning the taper. Or you can stand it on edge and straighten it as you go. If you do this, watch for folding at the thin edge.

Carbon steels such as those used for knives and chisels must be worked hotter than mild steel, or surface cracks can result. Remember not to let the carbon steel burn, though. If it does, you must cut off that part and start over.

Tapering an iron strap for, say, a door hinge involves drawing, which will upset and thicken the narrow part. You'll have to flatten it again to keep a uniform thickness. All this will lengthen your strap hinge a lot, so allow for it. I shape the tapered end with whatever decorative design I'm using, then cut off the wide end if it's too long when I'm through drawing it out.

This decorative end may require more iron than that left by the taper. You can upset, but that's the hard way. Leave a blob at the end as you draw to a taper if the design requires it. You've seen the classic spade or disc at the end of strap hinges on old doors. The smith usually flattened the decoration very thin, using just the iron at the end of the strap. That's one style. I like a uniform thickness, myself, which requires more iron.

A split curl or a three-way split can be done with the iron left in the strap. Cut back into the end with the hot cut or the hardy (it's hard to see what you're doing on the hardy because the cut is on the underside). Then bend all but one prong out of the way while you work that one to a point and curl it. Use the punch with the piece clamped in the vise to finish the cut, and bend the prongs out of the way. Cutting all the way through will dull the hot cut or hardy, even though this may be done on the table or step of the anvil, which is softer than the face.

Here's a good project to help develop control of the iron. We'll make a pot hook and nail for it all in one piece. Hammer a ⅜-inch round rod to a tapered point, then put a right-angle bend in it 2½ inches from the point, making the bend sharp at the outside. Now heat again and put the point through the nail heading bar and head just a little. Now cut off the rod 3 to 4 inches up, heat, taper, and form the hook. These are handy hooks for your shop, where you'll be more apt to have timbers to drive them into, or for kitchens with beams sturdy enough.

The same hook can have a loop, for a forged nail to be driven through into a beam. For conventional house walls, flatten the shank and punch a hole for a screw to mount it with.

Punching holes doesn't weaken the iron as does drilling them, because most of the metal stays in, pushed out to the sides. Also, punching is faster if you have the iron hot anyway.

Lay the hot iron flat on the anvil, then quickly drive the punch into it until you're almost through, when the cold anvil will cool the thin piece remaining. Now take out the punch and turn the iron over, with the hole right over the pritchel hole in the anvil. Drive the punch back through, placing it in the center of the outline you'll be able to see from the top.

The thin plug will drive out, and your hole will have a slight taper from both ends from the tapered punch. Now cool the punch in the

To make an integral pot- or coathook with forged nail for use in beams, draw to a point first, then bend a sharp right angle in. Next, head slightly in the nail heading bar, shown here.

The heading bar will allow a flat surface to hammer on when mounting the hook.

The stock is heated, cut off, and drawn to a point. Then bend it over the horn.

62

tub, and flatten the iron again on the anvil face. If this closes the hole a bit, punch it out again. If you want a bigger hole, heat again and use a drift (that's the big, tapered punch, usually with a handle) to enlarge the hole, over either the pritchel or, if too big for this, the hardy hole.

Your punch will get hot in thick pieces of iron, so remove between heats and cool it. You'll need to reshape, harden, and retemper it from time to time or it will mushroom and bend. If it mushrooms down in the metal you're punching, it'll be hard to get out. We'll discuss keeping your tools in shape in the chapter on tempering.

Riveting is a simple and effective way to join two pieces of iron. Punch holes and flatten the surfaces to be joined, then cut a piece of round rod a bit longer (⅜ inch or so) than the thicknesses of the two pieces to be joined. You should have a tight fit so the rivet will stay in place as you put the whole thing in the fire. The ends of the rivet will heat first, as you turn the piece. Now place the rivet end on the face of the anvil or on a riveting tool that has a rounded cavity in it, and use the ball-peen hammer to mushroom the top end. The bottom will spread on the anvil face, or will round in the riveting tool, and can be shaped more with the ball of the hammer.

I always have my students make several of their own tools in the

Complete the bend.

Heat and shape the tip. This makes it easier to hang a pot on, and also protects a coat from tearing on the sharp iron.

These hooks can be hammered into heavy beams, or into lighter wood if a lead hole is bored slightly smaller than the nail shank.

basic course I teach. Cold chisel and punch are the first, although we wait to harden and temper them till later. These are easy projects, involving only drawing and tapering, with rounding for the punch. I do stress that each piece of work should be shaped as much as possible with the hammer, leaving very little for grinding or filing.

Now let's go on to a more complicated tool, a pair of tongs for your own use. A good basic pair for light work would be about 12 inches long with flat jaws, to close with about ½ inch still open between the handles.

Use ½-inch square stock of low to medium carbon steel about 9 inches long. Cut two pieces and heat both in the fire at the same time. This lets you do each step on both as you go, and helps keep them uniform. Flatten 2 inches of the end of each to about ¼ inch thick, and round the corners. Now rotate the pieces 90 degrees, or to the next surface of the stock, and flatten the next 2 inches.

Now shape the ends of this second 2-inch flat surface at a long angle, using a flatter if you have one, or the side of the anvil tail if you don't. A flatter is a square-faced hammerlike tool that is struck with a hammer to shape the iron with more accuracy. You'll hammer a shoulder or step here, with the outside of each piece flush or flat its entire length, and the inside stepped to half the thickness, or ¼ inch, then back. Both pieces should still be identical. Hammer the shoulders till both pieces fit together as tongs should, then mark the pinhole with soapstone or with the center punch.

Punch both holes. I use a ¼-inch pin of spring steel because a bigger hole and pin can weaken the tongs. Now try a piece of pin stock through both halves to see how they operate. Make any necessary adjustments by hammering or grinding or both, but don't rivet the pin in yet.

You still have several inches of heavy ½-inch square handle to deal with. Heat and draw both to a long taper, which will stretch them considerably. They can be about ¼ inch in diameter at the ends, and should be somewhat less than the full ½ inch square even up near the flattened part at the pivot. Round the handles to a comfortable feel for you. I like an oval, so the feel of the handle isn't too sharp.

Now cut a pin of the spring steel, insert, heat, and rivet tightly. While still hot, force the handles apart and work them till the tongs cool. Don't quench to cool with the steel pin in or it'll become brittle.

For a blacksmith's finish on your tongs, heat to a black heat, which is just under darkest red, and dip into oil. It'll smoke and stink and maybe catch fire, so dip and remove quickly and hold downwind. The oil will penetrate the surface of the iron and turn it a nice black. Rub off excess oil with a rag as the iron cools. You may have to dip again several times if all the oil burns off the first time.

You may want to crosshatch the jaws of the tongs with a three-

FLATTEN, THEN TURN 1/4 TURN

FLATTEN

DRAW OUT AND TAPER

TWO OF THESE MAKE A PAIR OF TONGS

The finished tongs. A 120-grit aluminum oxide or carborundum sanding disc can be used to smooth the rough spots, as was done on this pair. Then they were heated to black heat and oil rubbed on them for a blacksmith's finish.

Forging a Pair of Tongs

(upper left)

Forging a pair of tongs: John Fitch, a participant in one of my workshops, holds the ½-inch square stock while I take a turn at the hammer. We're flattening the section where the pin will go, the jaw already having been shaped.

(lower left)

Al Lemons and I draw out the handle on a pair of tongs he's forging.

(upper right)

The small flatter allows a more exact flattening at the pin joint in the tongs.

(lower right)

This pair of tongs will have cupped jaws for holding round stock. A shouldering tool (a blunted hot chisel) is used on the jaw with it set into the step of the anvil.

The pin is cut hot from tough spring steel stock, so that a smaller hole and pin can be used. This steel is too hard to hacksaw.

The flattened matching face of this half of the tongs is punched for the pin.

The pin is heated while in place, taking care not to drop it into the forge fire, then riveted tight with the ball peen hammer. The tongs are then worked while hot to free them for use.

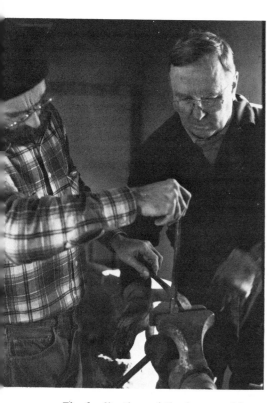

Final adjusting of the jaws and handles is done in the vise after riveting the pin. Any rough edges can be ground or filed now, too.

cornered file for better holding, but remember this will leave a pattern in the hot iron you handle with them. And you will notice a tendency for mild steel tongs to bend if you really clamp them tight, so you may want to use a better steel. I'd suggest ⅝-inch shafting, of about 30-to-50-point carbon, or maybe even reinforcing rod. These steels are tough instead of hard like higher carbon stock, and shouldn't need hardening for use as tongs.

I mentioned earlier that a favorite pair of tongs I have is made from horse hoof nippers with the jaws worn out—cheap at junkshops. Heat and straighten the jaws, and hammer till they meet with the right space open between the handles. Cut off any excess jaw on the hardy, since one will usually be longer than the other. These are high-carbon steel, so don't quench at all. They will cool in the air to a good, normalized toughness. And don't hammer the jaws at less than red heat, or burn them.

Another good learning project is forging your own hot cut, a very useful tool. We'll make it of medium carbon steel, since it always cuts soft red-hot iron. A section of car axle or large reinforcing rod or shafting will do nicely, about 1½ inches thick.

Punch the hole first, since this is an operation that can easily ruin the piece, and it's better not to have a lot of work invested at this stage. I punch the hole before I cut off the stock, which means I can hold it by hand for better control. Start about 3 inches from the end with a small punch, cooling often, and drive almost through as for any hole. Reheat when necessary, punch through from the other side, and drift out round. When you have a hole ¾ inch in diameter, flatten the spread outside of the bar to elongate the hole.

If you have an oval drift or handle drift, drive this in and flatten against it. If not, don't try to get the outside too flat or you'll distort the hole. The hole itself should taper from each end from the drift's having been used both ways.

Now heat the bar and cut off on the hardy about 3 inches past the hole, cutting from opposite sides. If you have hammerhead tongs, use them to hold through the hole in the piece. If not, use round- or square-grooved tongs on the end to draw the cutting edge to a taper. Leave some space between the taper and the hole so you don't distort it. Draw to an edge as you would for a cold chisel, and leave about ¼ inch thickness near the cutting edge, tapering back gradually. I go ahead and hammer the edge now, working at the edge of the anvil or on the horn so I won't dent the anvil face. Any time you miss the work and hit the hard anvil face with the hammer, expect it to bounce up into your face.

Once the edge is shaped, true up the struck end of the tool. Now let it cool in the air or in ashes to soften the steel, or anneal it. Air cooling is called normalizing and will work all right on medium-carbon steel. A thin piece of high carbon will harden in the air even without quenching, and be hard to file or grind. Burying the red-hot steel in ashes or in sand will slow cooling and make the steel softer, the annealed state.

Now grind the final shaping, or if you like shiny-smooth tools, file or polish on a belt sander. You're ready now to harden the cutting edge. If you're using axle steel or other medium carbon, just heat this edge to about an inch back, a cherry red, and quench in water. You should be able to mark it with a file, but not cut into it easily. If you've used a higher carbon steel, we'll tell how to harden and temper it in the next chapter.

The hot cut handle can be of anything, since it's used only to hold the tool in place when hit, not to swing it with. I pick up warped or otherwise imperfect seconds from handle mills or wherever I find them, two

Making a Hot Cut

(below left)
Punching the handle in heated stock for a hot chisel. It's easy to get the hole off-center and ruin the tool, so it's done first.

Cutting off the hot chisel stock on the hardy. Cut in the direction of the taper to be put on the tool.

Hammering to the tapered edge, using the hammer-eye tongs.

A finished hot chisel. This tool need be only medium carbon steel, since it only cuts hot metal. It's heated to cherry red and quenched only, since its carbon content is not high enough to make it brittle.

Filing the final edge on the hot chisel, after annealing. Rough spots can be filed or ground out at this stage.

for a quarter, for such tools. Sometimes I drawknife them from hickory or ash before the hearth on winter nights, along with the axe handles, cant hook handles, and others I use.

The heating and hardening of any tool you make will do away with the smooth shine you may have put on it during grinding or filing. If you want this on your tools, use the belt sander and perhaps a polishing wheel after hardening. The steel will rust easily, however, so keep a thin film of oil rubbed onto tools.

These are just some of the basic forging operations you'll use. Others we'll discuss as we go along. You'll develop your own approach to shaping iron and steel, and learn shortcuts yourself and from other smiths.

In the following chapters we'll go into more advanced techniques. In practice, stay with simple tasks until you master them, or your work will always be rough. There's nothing wrong with a primitive look to your forging, but you'll always feel like a beginner around another smith whose work shows more care and pride than yours.

CHAPTER FIVE

Tempering Steel

No area of working with metals is so laden with misinformation, ignorance, even downright superstition, as the hardening and tempering of steel. I recall an overgrown country boy back in the 1940s who refused to file the broken tip of his pocketknife blade.

"Why not?" I asked him. We were both about eleven and I'd say equally dull, but he'd just moved into that part of central Arkansas, and I figured he knew a lot of stuff. He was, after all, bigger than I was. Sure enough, he fixed me with a look of patient disdain, and I knew I was about to learn one of life's secrets.

"Because the steel in the file will draw the steel out of the knife blade. *Any*body knows that."

My estimation of this hulk dropped several notches. Had I heard right?

" 'The steel in the . . .' Aw, c'mon, now, you don't believe that!" He did. Fervently. Some old uncle or grandpa had told him, right out of the 1800s darkness of sharecrop farm belief.

Well, I finally succeeded in persuading the kid that the file could do no such thing, using the familiar use of files on axes and saws to illustrate. A light began to dawn.

"Well, okay, I'll file it, I guess," and off he went, mumbling to himself. "But if it ruins the blade," he called back, "it's your fault."

More common is the belief that heat will draw the hardness from steel (which it will) and that the tool is worthless from then on (which it isn't). Steel can be rehardened and tempered indefinitely.

I know an aging blacksmith who's better at hammering iron and forge welding than I'll ever be, who has a vast empty space in his knowledge when it comes to steel. I watched him punch holes in red-hot horseshoes, then reharden his punches (pritchels), which were of finest high-carbon tool steel, by coating them with case-hardening compound. Every time he used the tools, he heated them, applied the compound (which raises the carbon in steel), and quenched. Maybe he was trying to make diamonds or something.

The same man told me he could temper mild steel, which is so low in carbon that quenching has no noticeable effect on it. And a book currently in print has several paragraphs on the hardening and tempering of wrought iron, which by its nature cannot be hardened.

And an old codger my brother worked with on a horse ranch once had a stallion cut, to try to improve his violent nature. Apparently the veterinarian had forgotten his scalpel, and used a razor blade for the operation. The horse was still too spirited to be worth much, even as a gelding, and the old man blamed the use of the razor blade.

"Too high a metal in that razor," he swore. "Ruined that horse, usin' a razor blade on him." Lots of old-timers refer to carbon steel as being high in "metal."

Steel of a given carbon content is meant to do only limited jobs. I was at work in my village shop one day when a very old man stopped to watch. He'd been a country smith many years ago, and wanted to know if I ever sharpened plow points. Yes, I had, but there was not much need for that now.

"Well, I used to a lot," he remembered. "Draw 'em out if there was enough steel left, weld more on if there wasn't. Used to use a piece of car axle."

"On plow points?" I asked. Axle steel won't get very hard, being only medium carbon.

"Yeah, good steel, axles. And I thought I was a pretty good smith, y'see, could do just about any work."

"Well, I'm sure you were. But why'd you use axle steel on a plow point?"

"Good steel, axles. Only thing was, I never could get one really hard. Don't know yet what I done wrong."

All he did wrong, of course, was use a steel that couldn't do the job. Car axles must take impact and twisting, and are tough steel, not hard steel. The abrasion of soil and rocks on a plow point requires a high-carbon steel, like grader blade or jackhammer stem, or a piece of another plow point.

So: Let's simplify the complex and mystifying business of tempering steel, which is really a two-stage process. Steel is iron plus carbon, with some small quantities of other metals. The carbon in steel makes it harden when cooled suddenly by quenching from red heat or thereabouts. The amount of carbon in the steel determines the potential hardness. If allowed to cool in the air from the red heat, the steel is "normalized" or relatively soft, as we said in the previous chapter. If cooled slowly in hot ashes or in a dying forge fire, it's "annealed" or as soft and workable cold as it can be made.

TEMPERING STEEL — The Process of Heat Treating or Softening Hardened Steel to a Certain Level for a Certain Use

1. Choose a piece of steel to be worked for a certain purpose by its carbon content.
2. Forge the steel into the shape you need.
3. Heat the whole piece to red heat.
4. Quench. The whole piece is now glass brittle.
5. Grind a shine onto the surface of the portion of the piece to be tempered.
6. Return to the forge and carefully reheat the area to be tempered, watching the shined surface for the appearance of the four tempering colors which indicate temperature. The straw color, the first color seen, is coolest and leaves the quenched steel nearest its brittle state. Bronze indicates a slightly softer state. Purple is next. Blue is the hottest color leaving the steel nearest to normalized or soft. After blue, the steel goes back to the gunmetal color indicating that all hardness has been removed. At this point, if you have not tempered the portion of the piece the way you need to, you have lost your temper and must requench it (reharden) and reheat for the proper tempering colors.
7. When tempering colors start running, remove the steel partially or completely from the forge and let the proper color run to a stop at the proper place. DO NOT QUENCH.

Except for sophisticated alloys, steel, when heated to its optimum hardening temperature, usually cherry red, and quenched, gets as hard and brittle as it can be made. Some specialty steels, such as hard-surfacing welding rod, are designed to harden without quenching.

As I said, the quenched hardness depends on the amount of carbon in the steel. Now, a glass-hard tool, except for a file, is just about worthless, so the hardness has to be lessened to the right degree or "tempered." You don't temper steel to harden it; you harden it first, then temper to soften to the right toughness for the particular job to be done. Tempering steel hard is like slamming a door open, as blacksmith Wayne Haymes says.

Heat applied to the quenched, hardened steel softens the hard steel, making it tough instead of brittle. The degree of hardness/toughness is determined by both the original carbon content and by the degree of tempering heat applied. Sometimes the entire piece of steel is tempered, sometimes just part of it. Usually the working edge is hardest, and the rest (particularly an end to be struck with a hammer) softened through tempering more.

First let's go quickly through the heat treating process to establish the sequence, then we'll go back over it explaining each step as we go.

Heat the steel to a cherry red, then quench completely in the slack tub. Now the steel is hardest and brittle. Next shine the surface with a grinder, and lay it back in the fire. Heat slowly until tempering colors begin to appear. A straw color means the least amount of brittleness has been removed. Then bronze follows, with more heat, to take away more hardness/brittleness. Next is purple, then blue, the softest of the basic tempering colors.

All right, now let's detail the hardening of a piece of steel of 100-point carbon, which is 1 percent by content (high carbon). It could be any of several items, but for now it's just a piece of steel. Heat to cherry red, watching for a pulsing glow when held in the shade. That means the molecules are tearing around like mad in there, and the steel is at optimum quench temperature. You can see this color better if your smithy is semidark. Don't worry too much about the pulsing; some people never see it.

And that's just one way to determine the heat at which to quench. It's called the point of decalescence. Another way, probably better, is a graded quench: cut part way into a hot bar of the steel on the hardy at intervals about an inch apart, then heat from near white heat at one end, spreading the colors to dull red over several notches. Quench the bar in water. Now break off the first section, which will be quite brittle, by hanging it over the edge of the anvil and hitting it with the hammer. Remember the colors you heated to at the various notches.

You'll see a coarse crystalline structure to the steel at the white-hot break, getting finer as you approach the breaks at cherry red or near it. Use the color that gives you the finest, most satiny crystals at the break, whenever quenching this type of steel. It won't always be cherry red. And cherry red to you won't be cherry red to me or to somebody else. But we'll use that designation to simplify things.

While we're digressing, let me tell you another bit of useful information. Steel tends to weaken when heated above its quench temperature (the coarse crystals). So whenever you work it hot, as in welding, most smiths agree you weaken it. You can compact the structure of the steel and toughen it again by hammering it as it cools from the high heat, down past quench temperature. Don't hit it hard much below cherry red, or you can cause surface cracks. Cold-hammering too, helps toughen the structure.

Now back to that steel. Into the tub with the quench-temperature

Blue
Purple
Bronze
Straw

The tempering colors shown on this forged stone mason's hammer indicate the relative hardness of the steel. In this case, the flat striking face and the chisel end both need to be the hardest, or straw color, while the handle hole area must remain the gunmetal color or normalized state for toughness. The tempering process must be done in two separate steps concentrating on one end of the hammer at a time. After the whole hammer head was brought to red heat and quenched, the striking face was tempered. Then the top of the hammer was ground shiny to enable the blacksmith to see the tempering colors run clearly toward the chisel point. Heat for the tempering process was applied carefully toward the chisel end to avoid nullifying the previous process on the striking face. The straw color means less heat has reached the chisel point so that it remains the hardest.

A slightly softer bronze follows. Next is purple, then blue. Past the blue is a gunmetal color indicating the most heat has been applied here and resoftened the steel leaving it tough rather than hard. (See the back cover of this book for a color illustration of the running tempering colors from the chisel end.)

steel, to cool it as fast as possible. If it's a thick chunk, clear water is all right to quench in, from my experience. Other smiths won't quench thick steel in water, fearing contraction of the surface while the center is still fully expanded, causing cracking. I've never had this happen. If a thin piece, it is liable to crack in plain water. Again, some smiths use brine to slow the cooling and avoid cracking, some use it to speed the cooling. Pick your belief; I don't use brine at all.

An oil quench will definitely slow cooling, avoid cracking, and give a tougher steel not quite as hard as a water quench. Old motor oil is fine, although it will probably catch fire. You can cover it with a lid to smother it. You don't get maximum hardness quenching in oil, but sometimes it's a matter of keeping your piece in one piece. Do move the steel around in the liquid for faster cooling.

Now the steel is as hard as it can be, and 100-point steel can get hard. You won't be able to mark it with a file, and trying won't do the file any good. This hardness is too much for anything except maybe the cutting edge for a stone tool, or another file, but the piece is brittle, so now we'll soften or temper it for some possible uses.

Shine the steel with a grinder or emery cloth, and lay it back in the forge, over a slow fire. Eventually you'll notice a yellow glaze spreading. The color, an oxidation, indicates temperature only (it tells you hardness only in relation to the carbon in the steel). This yellow, or straw, will be followed by bronze as more heat is applied, followed by purple and then blue, with some shades in between. After blue there'll be a noncolor we call black heat, followed again by red if you leave it in the fire long enough. This whole process is called tempering, or "running the colors."

The straw glaze means we've softened the steel just a little: This is still good for stone tools; the steel is less likely to break. It is good for metalworking tools, too. Next is bronze—softer, but with 100-point steel, still hard. This is good for cold chisels, drills, where you want maximum hardness, but still some safeguard against shattering. Next is purple, better for wood chisels, punches, some knives, and for impact tools that don't need as hard an edge but get jolted a lot. (Tools that really get slammed around resist breakage better if they're of lower-carbon steel, by nature tough instead of hard.) Last of the oxidized colors is blue, softer yet, and still less apt to break. This is good for axes, knives, saws, hay hooks, fishing gigs, and springs.

Past the blues you've taken most of the hardness out and are close to normalized steel, which at 100 points is good for lots of things, too. A kitchen knife of this steel is plenty hard when normalized, and so are some springs and tools for working soft wood. There isn't much point in using such a high-carbon steel here, though. It still tends to be more brittle than tough, and a lower-carbon-content steel tempered to a color farther up the scale for about the same hardness would be better.

TEMPERING COLORS* and Their Effects on Steels for Typical Uses

	5 pt. (mild)	40 pt. (med.; impact)	100 pt. (high)	150 pt. (tool)
Annealed	No effect	Soft, like mild. Drill, grind, sharpen tools before heating. Use like mild.	Soft but tough. Drill, grind, sharpen before heat-treating.	Semi-soft; tough. Drill, grind, sharpen before heat-treating.
Normalized	No effect	Soft but tough. Drill, grind, sharpen before heat-treating. Use like mild; stronger.	Semi-tough. Use for kitchen knives, some springs, dinner gongs, tongs.	Tough. Hot chisels, drifts, forming pins.
Blue	No effect	Tough; will bend. Still relatively soft.	Tough, semi-hard. Axes, splitting mauls, knives, froes.	Hard. Hardies, cold chisels, punches. More brittle than lower carbon.
Purple	No effect	Tough. Tongs, triangle gongs. Tougher than mild.	Hard. Knives, some wood carving tools. Hot chisels, drifts.	Hard. Stone tools, drill bits, machine tools, plow points.
Bronze	No effect	Tough. Prybars, axes, saws, knives, shafting, splitting mauls, froes.	Hard. Hardies, cold chisels, punches, wood carving tools, augers, etc. A fairly safe temper for most tools.	Hard. Drill bits, machine tools, stone tools, files, rasps, plow points, some wear surfaces.
Straw	No effect	Semi-hard. Knives, wood carving tools, drawknives, hot chisels.	Hard. Stone tools, tools that should hold an edge but sustain no impact or bending.	Brittle. Files, some wear surfaces.
Quenched	No effect	Hard. Hardies, cold chisels, punches, wood carving tools, augers. Not as good as higher carbon.	Brittle. Edge only can be used on stone if rest of tool is tempered.	Too brittle for use.

*Remember, colors mean *nothing* unless carbon content is considered.

You stop the softening process at the proper color by taking the steel out of the fire a little before it's where you want it, since it will have a lot of heat left in it. If you've moved it around in the forge for even heat, you have an evenly tempered piece of steel. It'll tend to heat faster at thin places and at the edges. If colors run too fast, you can slow them by a quick dip in the tub, and your color will stop, and won't change until heat reaches that color at that spot again.

But be careful of this: Too many guides to tempering tell you to temper to color, then quench the whole piece to stop it. Such directions are an example of not enough information to serve well in actual practice. But if you're heating a punch, say, from the struck end, and get the bronze you may want at the tip, the other end will be much hotter, even red, and quenching to stop the bronze will make the struck end brittle, obviously.

Do apply tempering heat slowly. The heat must soak into the metal completely to be effective, and a quickly run temper will only affect the surface or thin parts of the tool, leaving the inside brittle.

If the colors change too fast, and you wanted a bronze but the steel goes to blue before you can stop it, heat to red and quench again, shine, and repeat the tempering. When the steel is the right color, you can quench quickly in and then pull it out to stop it without hardening a hotter part of it too much if you're very careful. We'll talk more about this later.

Heat-treating operations use ovens with high-temperature thermometers called pyrometers to get the proper hardness. It all depends on the carbon content of the steel, and the temperature it's reheated to after quenching. The oven treatment, used by most knifesmiths, gives an even temper all over, which is good or bad, depending on the tool.

Remember that, contrary to just about every set of directions in print, the tempering color chart on the back of this book doesn't tell you a thing about the state of the tempering *unless* you know the carbon content of the steel. And a piece of lower-carbon steel, if used in the experiment we just outlined, would change all the results in relation to colors. For example, 50-point quenched steel might have to be drawn not to a blue for an axe, but to a straw in order to be hard enough to hold an edge. The 50-point steel would be tougher, too, not having that extra carbon in it for more hardening potential.

We talked about finding steel in Chapter Three. The rule for a steel you aren't sure about is to quench and draw the temper (temper drawing is the complete name for the process) purposely to a color showing softer temper to ensure against breakage. You can reharden and draw to a harder color as use dictates, but if it's too hard at first, you break the tool and have to start over again.

Now let's apply this procedure to a practical tool—say, an axe made of, or resteeled with 80-point carbon (8/10 of 1 percent). Most automotive leaf spring steel, that old standby, is close to this. Heat the axe head to cherry red in the forge. It's not necessary to heat the entire axe, just a couple of inches from the cutting edge back, which will be the working part. We're assuming the axe was normalized or annealed from whatever forgework was done on it before. Get it hot slowly and watch for that flickering glow as it heats. If you don't see it, quench at what looks like cherry red to you. Quenched in clear water, the axe will be hardest; in oil, softer, but tougher. Let's quench this one in oil, which will guard against cracks as the quickly cooling metal contracts.

Now, don't even drop the axe while brittle or it might break. Use emery cloth or a grinder to shine a place from the edge back up the side of the tool. If you had a heat-treating oven and pyrometer, you wouldn't have to do this, but you have the forge and your eye. Lay the shiny axe in the forge over a low fire, or hold it up over the fire to heat it slowly, from the handle hole outward toward the edge. Turn often.

You'll see the light yellow or straw color spread over the shiny area toward the cutting edge. This will be followed by bronze, purple, and then blue. Heat slowly so these colors move out gradually. Rapid heating will cause a compact color band, hard on one side and soft on the other; with this combination the axe will tend to break in use. You want a band about 2 inches wide from straw to blue.

The colors are quite clear if seen in shade or low light. The colors are caused by oxidation on the surface of the metal, and only show up on the part you've ground down to clean steel. Stop the tempering as the first blue just reaches the edge.

Ideally, as we said, you should take the tool out of the fire ahead of time so the color runs out slowly, to stop at the right place by itself. You'll be able to do this easily in time, but you can lay the axe on the cold anvil to slow the run, or dip it quickly in and out of the slack tub; this is a bit tricky.

I routinely harden and temper tools such as axes in one operation. With practice, you will learn how to heat more than the area that it's necessary to quench. Now quench just the 2 inches or so of the working-edge area of the axe, leaving considerable heat back up toward the handle eye. Move the tool up and down in the tub to avoid a hot/cold line, which would almost certainly cause a break. Grind shiny with a stone or hone quickly, before the remaining heat can run down onto the part you've quenched. Use the heat left in the steel to run the colors, just as you would in quenching totally and reheating. Of course, this won't work with a tool to be tempered to an even hardness all over, but most tools should be softer and tougher back from their hard cutting edges.

Now, that same axe, tempered to blue, would be too soft if made of 30-point shaft steel, too hard if of 120-point quarry tool steel. You'd quench most shaft steel and draw maybe to a straw for the right hardness, or maybe not at all. The quarry steel you'd probably have to normalize in the air to keep it from breaking in use. Axes and saws take a lot of impact, distortion, and twisting in use, and must be softer than other cutting tools.

The same 80-point spring steel, made into a wood chisel, would be drawn to a bronze, much harder than the axe because it's less apt to break, being placed against the wood and struck on its softer end, or on a wooden handle with a mallet. The axe, swung often against hard knots and seasoned wood, gets some twists and jolts that require that the steel be tempered so soft that it's a rare axe that will hold a razor edge for long.

I have such an axe, which I steeled with spring steel and drew to purple for a harder edge. It's never cracked, but is too hard to file easily, so I use a stone on it. It doesn't need sharpening often, but I confess I fear that someday I'll chip it.

I tell you more about steeling an axe in the chapter on forge welding, but it's a tricky job. You may elect to do it with an arc welder. To do this, heat both pieces of steel to a dark red beforehand, and use a somewhat lower amperage setting than normal. Then cool slowly after welding.

One of the mistakes modern smiths make is the same one the old-timers made: They get hung up on the tempering colors and treat the tempering process as if all steel were of the same carbon content. I've had other metalworkers ask me what color to temper a hardy, say; of course, there's no set answer. A hardy of axle steel is not a hardy of jackhammer-drill steel, so the colors would be quite different for the same hardness. I happen to have a hardy made of each of these steels. The one made from the axle I just quenched; it wasn't temper drawn at all. The other is drawn to a purple. Accounts of early smiths tell definitely what color an axe should be, or a knife or a drill bit, with no consideration of the steel itself. And this is simply because they didn't know that the carbon content had that direct a bearing on the results.

You wonder how the old smiths, and even the modern ones, get even close with their tempering. Well, in time those who work with carbon steel a lot soon notice the differences and allow for them. Unfortunately, few of these craftsmen have written about the finer points of tempering for the guidance of the rest of us.

And in all fairness, there is less difference in steels that are, say, 20 points apart in carbon at the high end of the scale than there is at the low end. Twenty-point carbon steel and 40-point carbon steel are much more different than 80-point carbon steel and 100-point carbon steel.

Take the two examples we've just discussed, the experimental chunk of 100-point steel and the 80-point axe. These were close enough in carbon content to need approximately the same treatment for a not-too-different tool. An axe of 100-point steel would be a bit harder to file than one made of the 80-point steel if both were drawn to blue, and would hold an edge longer. But on a bitter January day, chopping a white-oak knot, a chunk might break off (this happened to me with a too-hard broadaxe just last winter).

Also, the steels available to the early smiths were less sophisticated than those today, and the demands of their clients less exacting. After all, there weren't factory-made tools of the same monotonous near-hardness available for comparison.

That old steel might and did have hard spots and soft places in it, and a host of other irregularities. Heating and hammering tended to spread and smooth out the rocky spots, giving more uniformity to it. So a belief still exists today that hammering iron toughens it. In the strict sense, this is not so. While lengthening the fibers or "grain" of wrought iron by hammering toughens it as iron, if the carbon was not in there, no amount of banging on it would put it in. Now, peening or hammering carbon steel will alter the crystalline structure of it, packing it and making it dense. This also relieves stresses in forged steel, and I often cold hammer a knife blade or other tool for this purpose. And we discussed hammering high-heated steel as it cools to toughen it again.

If you haven't followed this business of hardening and tempering, it's probably because there are so many aspects to it. Each smith learns to bend this or that rule a bit too, for the desired result, but he may not be able to tell exactly how he did it. Seldom will you heat, quench, and temper a piece of steel evenly throughout, or it would all be pretty simple. This is usually what happens to hardware-store tools. You'll want your tools hard at the working edge, tough through the shank, and softer at the struck end, if any, to prevent chipping or breaking, so this requires the more complicated hardening and tempering processes.

A difficult bit of tempering is a knife blade, partly because it's so thin, partly because, to get an even temper, concentrating the heat in the right places is quite exacting. We talk more about knives in the chapter on tools for your homestead, but let's temper a knife here.

Knifemakers usually work cold, grinding their shapes from flat stock, then heat treating evenly throughout in their ovens for a uniform almost-hard quality. They seek new and sophisticated alloy steels to allow for toughness, hardness, and corrosion resistance, all with a minimum of heat-treating effort. Most of them are loud in their condemnation of plain carbon steel for knives. However, my friend Frank Waite, a master knifesmith, creates beautiful, serviceable knives from new spring steel stock, as well as from the exotic alloys.

Carbon steel, hardened and tempered to the use for which the knife is intended, remains, after thousands of years, still the finest cutting edge we know. (I'm sure more than one metallurgist will disagree.)

A carbon-steel paring-knife blade is filed to final shape while annealed or softened by cooling slowly from cherry red.

After heating to cherry red again, the blade is quenched in oil to harden it, the first step in the heat-treating process.

The brittle, hardened blade, of 95-point carbon steel, is rubbed with emery cloth or a hone to shine it so tempering colors can be seen. Then heat from a very low forge fire draws the hardness, or tempers it to the proper degree, shown in oxidized colors. For the actual tempering, the blade is held in tongs and moved continuously in the heat for even tempering.

Let's use 50-point carbon steel, hot hammered to shape. You will have annealed the blade in hot ashes, to cool it over a period of hours, to its softest. Now you do whatever grinding and filing is necessary to remove humps, pits, and forging marks (if you want them removed). If you've forged carefully, there will be a minimum of cold work necessary. I draw file, pulling the file toward me for better control. Drill handle-mounting holes now, too, or thread the tang, which is the tapered end the handle goes on, if you plan to use a hollow handle and shaped nut to hold it on.

The blade will be so pretty now you won't want to put it back into the fire, but do so, moving it for uniform heat. Watch the tip and cutting edges; they heat faster. You can grip the blade by the tip with the tongs to slow heating there. Heat to cherry red, then quench, edge straight down, in oil. Period. Again, some smiths use brine, with enough salt to float a potato or an egg, but others insist this won't work. And clear water is risky. My nephew once spent four hours hammering a skinning knife from rare steel, then quenched in clear water. The knife cracked right across. Contracted too fast. Anyway, the oil will slow the cooling. You can quench in water by dipping in and out several times to slow the cooling, but you have to know just how. Hot water, too, will slow the cooling. Hell, just do it in oil.

All right, your shiny blade is gray now, and hard. And there shouldn't be any warp to it if you dunked it straight down. There might be some warp if you hammered too much on one side and not enough on the other in forging. If so, we'll straighten it later. Fifty-point steel is medium hardness, so you could conceivably leave the blade here. The chances are good that you'll break it, though. Shine it again with emery cloth, or on a belt sander if you have one, all over, making sure you don't get it hot enough to start colors running.

Now, 50-point steel is a tough metal, not a really hard one. You will temper to different stages for different uses. If after some use you find the knife too soft or too hard, you can remove the handle and reharden and retemper it. For general use I would draw to a bronze first. If this proves too soft, harden again and draw to light yellow or straw.

As we said earlier, it's relatively easy to temper evenly throughout, as most knifesmiths do in heat-treating ovens. In the forge you keep the blade moving over a low fire, watching to keep more heat on the thicker parts of the blade. The thin edge and point will go through the entire color range while you're waiting for straw on the back, or spine of the knife if you're not careful. Remove from the fire often, to slow the heating and for closer inspection. You may have to reharden and temper several times to get it right. Don't hurry, and banish onlookers during this process. More than one smith I know has burned up a good knife blade while answering a question.

A vegetable chopping knife my wife uses. It's of normalized spring steel, with forge marks left in.

Moving the knife constantly over the fire and turning it over often will make it easier to get the color even. For a graded temper, from hard at the edge to softer at the back, the procedure is similar, but more complicated. Heat from the back or spine edge, with the blade thin-edge-up over the fire, moving constantly and avoiding overheating the tip. Let the colors run from the back toward the cutting edge and toward the point. Heat very slowly, to spread the color band wide. A bronze at the cutting edge would be perhaps purple-blue at the spine. Let these colors run to a stop on their own. Dipping in water or oil to slow the colors will change the state of things enough to get you in trouble here, so I advise against it until you know what you're doing. Specifically, dipping will set the color run back, and new heat will run behind the band you stopped, but will not be visible as colors until it passes the previous band. Setting back the band by dipping, then honing a new shiny area so you can see the new colors, will not reharden a spot already softened or tempered.

The thin blade will cool quickly in the air, so your colors should stop soon after you remove it from the fire. I once hammered spring steel into a large kitchen knife for chopping vegetables. Experience had told me to normalize steel for this type of knife, so I let it air cool from red hammering heat. Later I decided to take off a bit more steel to allow for a longer handle. I clamped the blade into the vise to hacksaw it, and succeeded in dulling a new dollar blade. Moral: Carbon steel is tough and relatively hard even without heat treating.

Once your knife or other sharp tool is tempered, be careful about overheating it. It's true that it can be rehardened and tempered again and again, but this will mean removing the handle each time, and more close work. When grinding the blade, wet often to cool, and watch for those same tempering colors, which can come from the heat generated by the stone. Theoretically, if your tool is tempered to blue, you can let yellow, bronze, and purple appear while grinding, without changing the hardness. But grinding should be done more carefully anyway, and there's no point in letting it heat the tool that much.

About keeping blacksmithing tools in shape: Your punches and hot cuts and probably drifts and chisels will get dull, mushroomed at the struck end, and generally out of shape from frequent contact with red-hot iron. You can grind off flaring ends, or heat and hammer them back. Then reharden and retemper. Hammers themselves may mushroom with a lot of use, and they present a special tempering problem. The edges tend to harden, leaving a soft spot in the center of the hammer face. Harden under a stream of water, as from a hose, directed right into the face of the hammer. Then draw a little temper at the edges only. It's hard to get the face too brittle, since it's the edges that tend to chip. If you make a hammer, use high-carbon steel, not the medium of shafting or axle.

There are several points about hardening steels in general. Do draw the temper immediately after hardening, since with high-carbon steel, any good jolt can crack or break it in its quenched state. And hardening and tempering need to be extended only a short distance back from the working edge for most tools, leaving the rest normalized. And let tempering heat soak slowly through the metal. A quick run of color will temper the surface, but leave the core of the tool hard enough to break. A student of mine made a punch that was a thing of beauty, polishing it on the belt sander to a shine, tempering to just the right colors. But he ran his colors too fast, and the punch snapped an inch from the end in use.

Test stray or untried iron before you forge it, by at least heating to red, quenching, and trying a file on it, if not the graded quench we discussed earlier. I once hammered a link to join the hook to the body of a chain binder (boomer) and made the weld nicely, as a demonstration to a class. I cooled the work in the slack tub so everybody could inspect the weld, and everything was fine. But the first time I used the boomer, the link snapped clean, opposite (not at) my weld. I'd picked up a piece of carbon steel because it had been the right size. If I hadn't quenched it, the normalized steel could have been tough and strong. But I did and it became brittle, albeit nicely welded. The break came away from the welded point from the high heat (coarse crystalline structure). My hammering at the weld as the steel cooled toughened it at that point.

There's a bit more to this lesson. I was cinching a chain around my antique crawler tractor with the boomer when the link broke. I was getting ready to haul it on my log truck over some really bad mountain roads. I could have dumped the Cat off on somebody quite easily if that piece of steel had held only an hour longer.

The same thing happened with scrap bars I forged into a potrack for my wife. I'd put a decorative curl at the ends of two bars, then dipped them to cool for another handhold in forging. One wasn't quite nice enough, so I tapped it on the anvil horn cold for just a bit more bend. The whole curl broke off.

I often harden and temper tools with just the one heat, as we discussed about the axe. Here's another example, a cold chisel: Quench to about an inch, then dip deeper in and out, keeping the inch of the cutting end in the tub. While there's still some red heat up the shank, remove, lay across the anvil, and rub quickly with a hone or whetstone to shine. Heat will bleed down to run the tempering colors toward the cutting end. If these stop too soon, heat more; if they move too fast, slow with another quick dip in the tub or by laying on the cold anvil. This is not a good practice on very thin punches, because you get a normalized state for most of the length of the shank, and a thin punch will bend if used on thick metal.

By the two-stage process of hardening and then tempering, you will be able to control tempering colors better; for a wider band that means more toughness farther up the shank. Remember, you don't want hardness at the struck end, or steel will fly.

One-heat tempering takes practice, since the colors can run all the way off while you're shining the tool. And, of course, you can cool too much so there's not enough heat left to temper. The thing to watch most closely, though, is that tendency for a cold/hot line at the quench line.

I seldom try one-step tempering on such tools as double-bit axes, or, of course, on tools on which I want an even temper throughout. Until you get the hang of it (and remember that some very good smiths never do), stay with complete quenching, and a separate heat to temper.

You may find it difficult to control tempering heat in the forge. If you like, use a propane or acetylene torch to draw temper after you've quenched from forge heat. Or you can temper over a gas kitchen stove flame. Instead of the 1,500 to 3,000 degrees Fahrenheit of the forge, you need only from around 400 degrees to something over 600 degrees for tempering, once the steel is quenched.

With practice, you will be able to play the heat of your coal forge fire like a musical instrument, to get just the heat you need for any blacksmithing chore. And tempering steel is one of the two most exacting such jobs; forge welding is the other.

CHAPTER SIX

Forge Welding

Those photographs of colorful blacksmith types sending showers of sparks from steel hammered on the anvil are doing one of the most demanding tricks of the trade. Forge welding is about as difficult as tempering steel, although I know lots more older smiths who can weld than I know who can temper properly.

Joining two pieces of iron or steel by welding is simply heating to a temperature at which the surfaces of the pieces are molten, then placing them together and hammering them into one piece. And sometimes it works that simply. I recall the story told me at a Masons' meeting I spoke at. One of the older men there remembered trying to get an old blacksmith to teach the trade to CCC workers in the Depression.

"Don't know what I c'd teach 'em," he said, spitting tobacco juice reflectively.

"Well, teach them to make things, fix things. Teach them to weld."

"Don't know how I'd teach 'em to make stuff," he shook his head dubiously. "Nothin' to it, just make it."

"How about welding? That's certainly difficult. You could teach that."

"On'y thing I know to do is to get the iron hotter'n hell and beat the devil out of it," he said. "Can't teach that."

And he was about right. Of all the aspects of smithing, forge welding seems the hardest for students to get, and do consistently. When hardening and tempering are explained logically, students usually pick it up fairly well, but welding is another thing. And it's really no wonder. Taken step by step, the procedure has a lot of ways to go wrong. A lot of things must be right before that heat and that hammer can make two pieces one.

The thing that rattles most smiths about welding is the time factor. Faced with a task that must be performed in seconds if at all, a lot of folks panic.

There's the steel. Wrought iron worked easily and welded easily in the old days. Even steel welded to it easily. The mild or carbon steels of today seem to oxidize faster and are harder to weld. Also, steel burns easier at the high temperatures required for welding, fed by the blast of oxygen-laden air.

Then there's the coal. Dirty coal—that with high sulfur, that which leaves you with large clinkers—won't allow a decent weld. The crude metal clinkers melted out give off oxides, I'm told, that inhibit welding. And that is doubtless the reason, since an old blacksmith's practical joke was to visit another smith and drop a copper penny down into his forge when his back was turned. He wouldn't be able to weld all day, and of course wouldn't know why. Bits of stray nonferrous metal in the forge will keep you from getting a weld today, too.

The pieces to be welded must be shaped so that, when hammered together, the oxidation scale between them is driven out, to leave clean iron to flow together. This shaping is called scarfing, and the simplest weld is a lap scarf, in which one piece is tapered to overlap the other, also tapered. The resulting bond is thicker than either piece, and shaping the welded joint reduces it to size. Some smiths first upset the ends for still more iron to work with after the weld is made.

The oxidation scale, which can be reduced by the use of a welding flux, probably prevents more forge welds than any other single factor. Some dexterous smiths have developed a lightning-fast swipe of the white-hot iron surfaces with a wire brush just before the surfaces are welded. Others tap the iron against the anvil to knock scale off. If the scarf is properly made (and the coal is clean and the fire deep and the heat right, and if some other factors are favorable), the scale is effectively driven out with the first hammer blow.

A chain link is a simple beginning weld to make, since you're welding one piece of iron back to itself. It'll hold itself in line, properly heated, instead of requiring some sleight-of-hand to get it all together on the anvil one-handed while you grope for your hammer, all before it cools in the second or two you have to work.

Scarf the ends of the rod, which should be ⅜-inch round stock, about 7 inches long, to give you room to work. That'll make a nice, long link. Bend into an oval, with the scarfed ends overlapping maybe ⅜ inch. The scarf is more than a simple taper; it should be rounded so that the iron will touch in the center first, to drive out the scale better. Now use welding tongs, something with a cutout in the jaws to hold the link opposite the joint, and heat to red. Sprinkle flux on to inhibit oxidation. Borax is the base of most welding fluxes; some smiths use borax and sand. Some use just sand. Some sprinkle iron filings in, too. The melted flux flows

Blacksmith Wayne Haymes shows a student chain welding. The weld has just been made, and the joint is being shaped on the horn.

over the surface of the iron, sealing it from oxygen with a crude kind of glass, as it heats.

Now back into the fire, which should be a deep, clean one—no clinkers. You should clean the fire before welding, even if it means taking it completely apart and building another one. With a good grade of coal and a clinker breaker in the firepot, a twist of the handle will clear the fire. Then repack it and mound coke up high. Bring the joint to white heat fairly quickly, since slow heat will heat the entire link, and it'll spread when you hit it, instead of welding. And heat fairly high in the fire to reduce oxidation. Watch for a very light yellow, which is as white as the iron will get without burning. You can cheat a little with mild steel and leave it in the fire till the first white sparks come off. The iron is beginning to burn here, and a little of this won't hurt much. Carbon steel must never be allowed to burn even a little or the piece is ruined: It crumbles apart.

All right: You're probably right-handed, so you're turning the blower with your left hand. Shift the tongs to the left hand, take the link out, turn to the anvil where your hammer should be, lay the link flat down on the face, and hit it quickly three or four times—not too hard, but firmly. Sparks will shower as droplets of molten iron spatter and hot scale flies. You'll see the joint bond by the second stroke or so, and then you

This forge welding picture shows why a leather apron and even a hat are important. Those streaks are molten iron drops and bits of white-hot scale.

can hang the link on the horn to shape the weld while it's still hot. If the weld didn't happen, don't waste more hits. You can reflux and heat again if you didn't distort the scarf too much. If you did, reshape both ends and try again.

About those sparks: I once burned little holes in a photographer's stretch pants while she was getting pictures of a weld. I'd get a leather apron made at a craft shop. Mine comes clear up to my neck. Also, a hat will keep the odd spark out of your hair.

I weld at a very high heat, just a few degrees short of burning, and have fair success. I know smiths who can and do weld at what I'd call an orange heat, and do it well. The secret (one of them) is to have everything in place so you don't waste any time and heat.

One of my students went on to become the smith at a historic attraction, and became a good ironworker. He had trouble with his welding, though, and finally called me to come to see what he was doing wrong.

Well, his coal was the best I've ever used. His forge and tools were mostly new, and good. I watched him shape a chain link, and he did it just as I'd taught him. His heat was right, too, but he laid the link on the anvil, tapped it once lightly to sort of get it located, then took his time getting on it with the hammer.

Well, of course the cold anvil face takes the heat out very quickly. If possible, you should even hold the iron up off it until you're actually swinging the hammer. We corrected that hammering and he made one good weld after another. Tourists gathered around, so I had him weld separate pieces. Then I had him weld a bundle of rods (this always looks impressive). He did that, too. As far as I know he's doing well, years later.

Your chain link will still be egg-shaped after welding, so shape it with the weld at the end. That way part of each end goes around and it holds better. Commercial chain is usually welded electrically at the sides, and that's where it breaks. We'll discuss chain more in the chapter on homesteading tools.

A hoop is another good beginning weld, made on the anvil horn. Scarf the ends, and leave a little tension in to hold the joint together. Some smiths even punch holes and rivet first, to help get a good weld. Old-timers used to pride themselves on their smooth welds, challenging anyone to find the joint in a welded wagon tire. They often used more than one heat, and of course were working with wrought iron.

Shad Heller of Branson, Missouri, taught me to forge weld, and his advice was to walk through it cold a few times, to know exactly where the hammer was, just how far to zip the iron to the anvil, and so on. It helped a lot. One freak happening in courses I've taught is that of a rattled student picking up the hammer backward, and slamming the weld with the peen. Now I keep a double-face hammer to teach welding with.

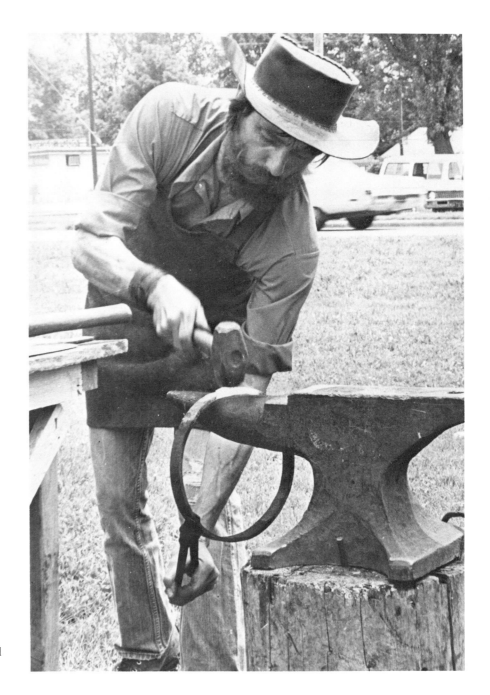

A hoop weld, showing finishing and shaping of the thickened weld.

A tricky weld to make, and one always harder than it looks, is the eye of a froe, that shake-riving tool of antiquity. I've seen lots of old specimens doubled for the length of the blade, and I know it's not really evidence of top craftsmanship; that smith had trouble with the weld, too. You see, it's actually easier to shape the eye, double the thickness of the blade, and start the weld at the tip, progressing back toward the eye. Simply welding near the eye is harder, especially with high-carbon steel, which burns easily.

This is a tool that should be struck only with a wooden mallet, and need not be high carbon, but most smiths make the froes from leaf spring, which is apt to burn near welding heat. Flattened axle steel welds easier, and makes a tough enough froe if you want to put in the work required.

Anyway, the problem is that the steel around the loop, and the thin scarf edge, tend to get hotter and burn before the heavy body of the blade gets to welding heat. Keep the body down, turning only after it's up to heat, and watch that the edge of the eye doesn't burn. Hammer the end of the scarf first, before the thin steel can cool, then work back toward the eye with very rapid blows, aimed first at the center line of the weld. That helps drive out the scale. There's nothing wrong with taking a second heat for this weld, which is usually about a 2-by-3-inch area.

I've seen other ways around this weld. One of the most effective, but just as hard, I'd say, is splitting the steel to form both halves of the eye, and hoop welding at the back on the horn. Some smiths punch a hole in the blade body, shape a tenon (a rounded protrusion, like an attached rivet) on the end of the eye loop, and rivet it through. Some don't even weld the eye at all. Others punch matching holes and rivet the lap before welding. This technique will help you get this weld, but remember to leave the joint open out from the riveted center, to get flux in and scale out.

You probably won't weld many froes, since there's so little good timber for split shakes these days. But I do a good trade in froes, both at fairs and as special orders. I suspect that most of them never rive a shake, but are included in old-tool collections, where they're bragged about as being definitely hand-forged, and lied about as being old.

Recently I saw a froe that had been made in an old country shop years ago, and that had a nice touch to it. The smith evidently didn't like the fact that, no matter how sharp the bend from the eye to the blade, a little triangle is always left open. He'd laid a wedge of iron in there and welded it along with the lap weld. Nice.

If you weld any high-carbon steel such as spring steel for a froe or new steel on an axe, keep hammering as it cools down past quench temperature. This will pack the steel's crystalline structure, which will have become coarse and weakened from the high welding heat.

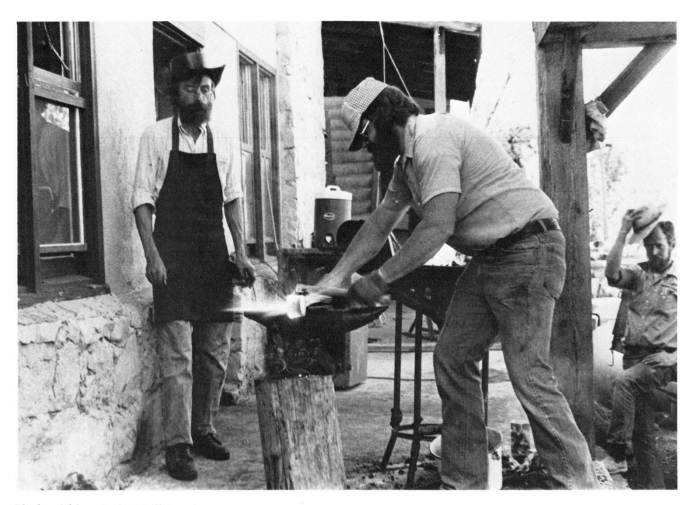

Blacksmithing student Bill Jennings
of Branson, Missouri, makes the
weld at the eye of a froe, a tool for
splitting shakes.

Graduating from welding a single piece back on itself to welding two separate pieces is a big step. Unless you rivet first, a lap weld means that the two pieces are loose until you weld them, and hard to manage without a helper. You heat them side by side, keeping the heat even in both, then bring them out and lay the one in your hammer hand face-up on the anvil, tipped up so the cold face won't contact the iron, then push the piece down with the other piece, face down, as you swing the hammer. If your heat is right, you can touch the two together in the air and they'll stick slightly, letting you have a fraction of time to position them before they go on the anvil.

If the pieces are long enough to hold by hand, it's easier. Any forging operation is harder if you have to hold the iron with tongs.

A trip-hammer is handy here. You can hold the pieces together and let the machine pound them together, controlling it with your foot.

As I said earlier, it's easier to weld if you've managed to get the joint held together somehow beforehand, as with the rivet. Splitting one end to enclose the other is another way. I steel an axe head by shaping the carbon steel bit to a vee, which encloses the old axe edge. Then I use a center punch on the hot steel to make little indentations to help hold the steel in place for the weld. I flux before I drive the new steel over the old.

The early smiths, having little steel, did it the other way when they made an axe. They folded a piece of wrought iron around a handle shape, then welded it double up to the edge, leaving a vee for the steel bit, which went inside. With spring leaf so plentiful, I find it easier the other way. Just lap welding steel onto a worn axe is a hard weld to make. I suppose riveting might help here, too, but I have never done it.

The part of the weld joint that touches the anvil will lose heat quickly, and usually leave a crease where the thin edge of the scarf got too cold to flow. You can minimize this by getting the first, telling blows in on one side, then flipping the piece over quickly to smooth the other side. It still won't flow together, but will be less noticeable. You can take a second heat on this side.

A light piece of iron loses its heat quickly, so you have proportionately less time to work. Heavier pieces hold heat longer. Old forged anvils were welded twice, with two strikers and sometimes more, alternating sledgehammer blows. One weld joined the two sections of the anvil body; the other joined the hard steel plate that formed the face.

Shad Heller tells me the story of what is supposedly the biggest forge weld on record. It seems that a steamboat broke a 6-inch-square paddle-wheel drive shaft on the Mississippi River near Memphis many years ago, and the captain wanted the drive shaft welded. No ordinary smithy could handle it, of course, but the owner of a large shop finally agreed to try. The two halves were slung from chain hoists overhead, so they could pivot from two forges to the giant anvil. They were scarfed, heated,

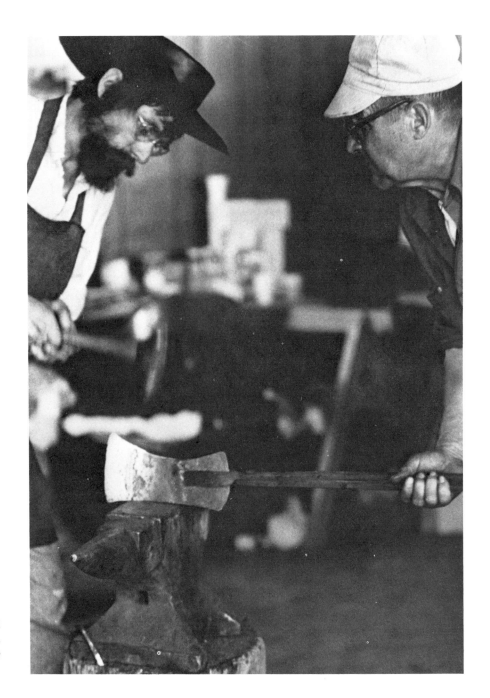

Steeling a double-bit axe. The weld
has been made, spreading the blade.
Here we're shaping it back. Later we
welded steel onto the other edge.

fluxed, and then brought to white heat, as four strikers, positioned exactly, waited. Then the balanced shaft pieces were swung from the forges to lap just right on the anvil, and the strikers rained blows in perfect time, to make the weld. The shaft held on the trip upriver, where it was eventually replaced.

Old books on blacksmithing caution welders to align the grain in iron before welding. That was more important in wrought iron than it is in modern steel, since the fiber of the iron definitely ran lengthwise. The grain of mild and carbon steel is less obvious, these being more crystalline in nature. But it's still a good idea. Some old iron is especially prone to split when forged, which can be the result of rust getting into the grain.

It's safe to say that no welded joint is as strong as the iron on either side; this was an axiom in the old days. With arc or acetylene you can build up more metal than is on either side for strength, but a forge weld depends on those two faces hammered together, and that's all.

Weaker still than the scarf weld are the butt weld, in which the two ends of pieces are hammered together, and the jump weld, with an end hammered onto the middle of another piece. Wherever possible, you should forge from a single piece of iron and not depend on a weld or a joint of any kind, particularly at a stress point.

All those neat drawings of complicated welds in old blacksmithing guides are nice, and there was no practical way to join those pieces except by forge welding. But trying some of them with today's materials will be an exercise in frustration.

For those who never get the knack of welding, there are lots of ways around it. A chain hook can be of bar stock, or my old standby, a railroad spike, with the hole punched in instead of looped and welded. In ornamental work, a rivet often joins quite well, without the awkwardness of getting the piece into the fire, or the distortion of hammering the weld. A band, too, applied hot to cold pieces, will contact on cooling to hold well. And often a small punched hole can be drifted out and enlarged on the anvil horn to a loop as large as the amount of metal will allow, letting you avoid a weld that way.

I will not weld an axle or drive shaft, reasoning that the stress that broke it will do so again. With steel as abundant as it is now, it's safer to replace shafting. Similarly, when I'm faced with welding steel into a plow point or digging tool, I'd rather forge a new one. Unless the shape is complicated, the new piece is as quickly shaped, and is stronger.

I will say this about forge welding: Compared to arc or acetylene, it is often a superior weld. First of all, it is impossible to forge weld without preheating both pieces, which makes any weld better. It's common to arc weld carbon steel, and have it break right next to the weld. Preheating, welding with the right rod, and heat treating will stop this. Acetylene welding allows better preheating, but again the rod used to join the pieces must be of the proper carbon content for a strong weld. With the forge weld, there's no rod, so you work with the iron you have.

Ideally, any joint to be welded in any way should be heated at least to red beforehand, welded, then cooled very slowly. If carbon steel, the piece should be hammered while cooling, then hardened and tempered again to its use.

Welding will continue to be fascinating to most folks. I recall a man telling me recently of an old smith back in the mountains who was a real wizard at his craft. Seems he'd been off to the Smithsonian Institute or somewhere to demonstrate, according to my informant.

"You know, that old man can even forge weld," he told me, in evident wonderment. (This man didn't know that I, too, was a blacksmith. He'd have thought I was too young anyway, merely middle-aged.)

Well, he finally mentioned the old codger's name, and I recognized it as belonging to a colorful smith of the horseshoe variety who looked a lot better than he was. In fact, this same old man had asked another smith, a friend of mine, to teach him forge welding just a year or so before, probably so he could demonstrate it for those historians.

But I didn't let on. "A dying art," I agreed. "Too bad he couldn't teach some of that knowledge to somebody who'd carry it on."

"Nobody's interested these days," my man snorted. "Anyways, that forge welding's too hard. Why, it took that old man most of his life to learn that. I just imagine that secret will die with him."

"Probably will."

CHAPTER SEVEN

Tools for Building

Being a hewn log house builder/restorer, I consider a cross cut saw, axe, froe, broadaxe, auger, and drawknife the kinds of building tools that are essential. Of these I have forged all but the saw. And for my kind of construction, the saw is perhaps the least essential.

Whether you plan to build of logs, stone, post-and-beam, or conventional studwall, your forge can help fill your toolshed with handmade or rebuilt tools that you'll treasure and get good use from. Let's look at a proposed building project—a timber-framed barn—and the tools you'll need.

First of all, there'll be the site preparation, if only some leveling of the dirt floor. An old, worn pickhead can be had at a junkshop, often for a dollar or less. Draw out the pickhead and sharpen it, then quench and temperdraw to a dark straw so the tips won't break. Then find yourself a handle. I drawknife mine from shagbark hickory or ash. Making a pick or shovel from scratch is the sort of thing that'll keep you from ever getting to work on your barn, so save that work for tools you really can't find cheap. And when looking over old pickheads, find one with as much metal left as you can. You can forgeweld new steel on, using, say, large coil spring steel, but it's a tough weld to make, in a place that takes a lot of stress.

Once level, your site may need stone shaped a bit for the foundation. I make an odd-looking stone-dressing hammer by wrapping a piece of high-carbon steel, like a heavy truck leaf spring, around a handle drift, forge welding it, drawing to an edge, then serrating while it is annealed. Use a large three-cornered file to make the teeth. This may be too much for you to tackle, so shop around for a stone hammer, or use a stone chisel. The stone hammer is really just a chisel with a handle. If you forge a hammer or a chisel, barely draw the temper from the cutting edge; stop the straw color as it reaches there. Do draw temper from the rest, to a normalized state at the struck end if a chisel. A really hard edge backed closely by tougher steel will handle stone best.

HEAVY STONE HAMMER

FOLD AND WELD

SERRATE WHILE ANNEALED

TOOL STEEL— 100+ CARBON

LIGHT MASON'S HAMMER

A good small stone hammer can be shaped from an old hammer head. Without the hole to punch for the handle, it's a lot easier. A large ball peen will do, and you can draw either the ball out to a short chisel shape, as in a cross-peen hammer, or the striking face out to a longer one, shaping the ball to a flat striking face. Put a slight curve into the chisel shape, since your swing is in an arc. Leave an edge somewhat like that of a cold chisel, since the tool is used to chip or break stone, rather than cut it, and should be a little blunt. Draw the temper to a straw from the eye toward both the working face and the edge, letting it go to the face, but stopping it ¼ inch short of the edge. This is a bit of a trick if you do both at the same time. You can dip one end to keep it cool while running the colors on the other, then reheat and reverse. The stone hammer on the back cover of this book was forged from scratch, but that's what it should look like.

Now back to the barn. If you plan to hew beams, you may not be able to find a broadaxe you can afford. They are collectors' items just now, and I rarely see one that costs under $40. An adze is cheaper, but this is a finishing tool and won't do much toward squaring round logs.

I have forged new steel onto the cutting edges of worn broadaxes,

A completed McRaven broadaxe, with some forge marks still showing. The head is mild steel, wrapped around and welded, with a poll added, and carbon-steel edge, tempered to blue, of 95-point steel. The axe is handled for right-handed use.

and made them completely from plate steel. Let's say you've found an old axe with most of the metal sharpened away. You can weld a piece of spring leaf onto the cutting edge, draw out, sharpen, quench, and temper it, and have a usable axe, probably for the rest of your life.

As we discussed steeling axes last chapter, it's not an easy weld to make. I suggest folding the new steel to leave a slot for the old cutting edge to fit into, then welding. If forge welding isn't one of your smithing skills, or if you can't find clean coal, torch or arc weld the new steel on. Do heat both pieces of steel first. Or you can butt weld, after grinding the old edge blunt. If you forge weld, you won't be able to get all that steel hot at once, so weld a couple of inches at a heat. Wire brush the scale off between heats, and reflux each time.

One thing to watch for in tempering a broadaxe is warping. This seems to be a result of hammering more on one side than the other, or of uneven heating. If you use a steel of 80 to 100 points, you may find that simply aircooling or normalizing it will give you all the hardness you need. The broadaxe is used to slice off wood with the grain, as opposed to chopping across it, as with a timber axe, so it can be softer and still do the job.

If your broadaxe, of 80-point steel drawn to a blue, does warp, you

1/4" CARBON STEEL BAR
ABOUT 2" X 5"

FOLD

HAMMER EDGE

AXE AND HAMMER
EYE TONGS

STEELING AXE

DRAW AND SHAPE

QUENCH AND DRAW
TEMPER TO PURPLE / BLUE

FORGE WELD AT
WHITE HEAT

can coldhammer it straight but carefully. Lay the axe head flat on the anvil face if the axehead will lie flat (there's usually a slight arch across the anvil face from side to side), or on a curved surface such as grader blade or railroad rail if it won't. Hammer evenly all over the convex surface—lightly at first, then heavier if the warp isn't coming out. Don't do this with steel hardened to a brittle stage. You can also hammer life back into sagging spring leaves this way, cold.

The same steeling procedure—forging new steel onto worn edges—works well with single- or double-bit timber axes. I have one of each I've reclaimed this way, and have done several for others. A better steel for high-impact work is automotive axle, but the hammering takes a lot of time, unless you have a trip-hammer. You can, of course, go to a steelyard and buy some thin bars of 30-to-40-point carbon steel, just right for the job.

I'm reminded of that blacksmithing student of mine who wanted to make a Bowie knife that he could throw without fear of breaking. Partly to give him a conversation piece, I had him cut 5 inches of axle steel and handed him the hammer. Many hours later he'd reduced that 1½-inch bar to a beautiful 11-inch blade, drawfiled it to perfection, and will probably pass it on to his grandsons, along with the story.

With your barn beams hewn, you'll need to mortise and pin them into place. Woodworking chisels are easy to forge, and certainly more satisfying to use than the plastic-handled commercial variety. I use coil-spring steel, temper drawn to a bronze. Leaf spring is good, if you have a shear to cut it to size. I make chisels in sets, using spring bars of a suitable diameter for each. A ⅝-inch bar will give you plenty of steel for a 1-inch mortising chisel; I use ¼ inch for sculptor's finishing chisels. As with any carbon steel, hammer it hot but don't burn it. I use a shouldering tool or the edge of the anvil to step down to the tapered handle tang, then fit a heavy, square-hole washer to it for the wooden handle to seat against. Quench and temper draw from the tang to a bronze at the edge, stretching your colors out to at least an inch-wide band. I notch the tang to hold better, drill the handle with a tapered metal bit, and drive it on dry. You may want to use epoxy glue, too. The handle itself is, for my tools, perhaps a rare piece of tiger-stripe hickory, or maple or elm. Sometimes I will use a hardwood inclined to split, like Osage Orange, and band it with iron or brass. The mallet should be hardwood; dogwood or persimmon are favorites in my region.

I often adze or drawknife beams to smooth them after hewing. A drawknife is a tool with so many uses that you should have several sizes. A 12-inch cutting edge is handy, although I've made them as small as 4 inches and up to 18 inches.

A split spring leaf is the simplest steel to use; cut on the shear to about an inch width. If none is handy, I sometimes use coil spring, which

This drawknife was made of medium-carbon shaft steel, heated and quenched only. The relatively low carbon content kept it from becoming brittle and produced a tool of toughness with just this one-step process.

takes a lot of hammering. Leave 2 inches or so of steel at each end for the tangs, and hammer the tool straight. Hammering the cutting edge will curve your drawknife, and leave some of that curve in. It will slice better than a straight edge. Now draw the tangs, allowing about 8 inches for the bends and handles.

I leave the tangs square, and drill the handles through, to fit a square-hole washer, which I round with the ball peen, and rivet over the tang ends. The square shape helps keep the handles from twisting when driven tight onto the tapering tangs.

After I've quenched the tool, I draw evenly to a bronze or purple. Then I draw all the hardness from the tangs, because they tend to break at the bends if hard.

I use round pole rafters in many of my buildings, and the drawknife is handy to peel the bark. So is a barking spud, but this is a tool of limited use unless you plan to build completely of round logs. Half a post-hole digger, sharpened, works well as a barking tool, too.

To drill for the wooden pins, or trunnels, you'll need a set of augers or bits for a hand brace. These can be made in the forge, but are really cheap at junkshops. To forge them, use a medium-to-high-carbon steel—again, spring steel is good—and hammer it uniformly flat, to about ⅛ inch thickness. You can find spring steel leaves this thin, and cut them with the shear to the width desired; a 1-inch width results in a 1-inch auger. Leave a shank, hammered to a square taper.

Twisting the auger is one of those delightfully simple processes involving hot iron and a vise, that always seem to come out right. The trick is to heat uniformly. Now straighten any bends the twisting might have produced. File your cutting edges while the steel is annealed, and thread the tapered point with a three-cornered file. This is a close operation, so take your time. Heat to cherry, quench in oil, and draw to bronze or purple.

I like the T-bar auger for large holes because you can really get leverage on it. The brace is fast for small work, but if you're boring through, say, a white oak top plate and the hewn log beneath it, a 20-inch hole 2 inches across, you need torque. I shape a metal plate to take the square-tapered shank of the bit, recessing this plate into the handle and fastening with screws to it. At the top another plate with a smaller square hole is recessed, screwed down, and the shank end riveted over it. Bits get wobbly and fall out if they're not anchored tightly. Hickory and ash are my pet woods for auger handles.

With your rafters pegged into place, you're ready to slat and shingle your barn. While I often forge nails for decorative purposes, I don't advise investing the time to do it for general construction. I do often forge extra-long heavy ones to pin the rafters to the plates. Sometimes these are a foot long, of medium-carbon steel such as reinforcing rod,

THREAD WITH DIE

T-BAR AUGER

TWIST IN VISE WHILE HOT

SHAPE CUTTERS AND THREADS WITH 3-CORNERED FILE WHILE ANNEALED

sometimes started in a smaller drilled hole to keep from splitting the rafter.

Nail down the slats or laths the shingles go on, with good old 10D common nails. But you will want to rive your shakes if you can find good wood that is straight, with no knots. That's often disappointing these days, but now and then some good second-growth red oak, white oak, or even large cedar will be available.

So you need the froe. This is a very easy tool to make if you don't care how it looks; it's harder if you do. Use heavy spring leaf, hammer it to an edge, and loop an eye in one end for a handle. Let it cool normally. That, with a handle, will give you a useful tool for splitting shakes or

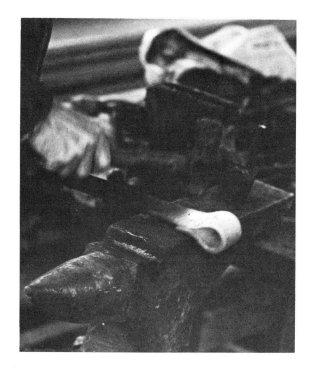

Bending the eye of a froe in leaf spring steel on the anvil horn. This tool is used to split or rive shakes or boards from straight-grained wood.

(upper right)
The tricky froe-eye weld can be made easier by riveting beforehand, using the ball-peen hammer. Or the froe can be used nicely with just the riveted joint.

The froe-eye weld, made after fluxing with borax at red heat, then heating to white welding heat carefully, turning often so as not to burn the steel.

slats. If you want to make it authentic, you'll have to make that weld we talked about earlier.

There's yet another way around the froe-eye weld if you want to take the time. I'm a believer in one-piece forgings wherever possible: shaping the iron without joints of any kind. You can punch a hole near the end of the froe, then drift it out larger, and finally shape it around a piece of shafting, axle, or the anvil horn, twisting the blade one-quarter turn for the finished froe. It takes a lot of hammering, and the sides of the eye will be thin, but it works.

Barns need hinges for doors, latches and hooks and heavy nails to hang things from, and chain to lift things with. Chainmaking is the crafts-center blacksmith's stock-in-trade. Chainmaking is fast, requires enough skill to look good, and is a bona fide activity. And it's good practice. But it's really not economical unless you count your time for nothing.

Hooks are another matter, since they're expensive, and somehow usually absent from the scrap of chain you found along the road or bought at the flea market. A hook should be much thicker than the chain it's attached to, since the hook is open and can be pulled straight with less force than it takes to break the chain. I sometimes punch the hole that links the hook to the chain. A forge weld here is not difficult, either. The thing to remember is to shape the hook before you bend it, be it a curved slip hook or slotted grab hook.

Of course, other building jobs would require other tools, not all of which you'd want to make at the forge. I suppose I could hammer out a saw if need be, since this is the way they were made for centuries, but times will have to become much harder before I try it.

The same is true of hammers. I have forged hammers of several types, but the truth is that you can pick up whatever you need quite cheaply at the junkshop.

A wrecking bar is a handy tool that can also be had cheaply, but is quickly made at the forge. I use coil spring steel from ½ inch to 1 inch in diameter, heated and straightened. Flatten both ends to chisel points, then split the one end with the hot chisel, working from one side to leave a sharp tapered edge. Bend the curved end toward the open taper of the split. Quench, and draw to a purple or blue. A harder temper will break if you hammer on it, and you will, eventually. Two or three of these tools, from 1 foot to 3 feet long, will be useful in any kind of building or dismantling. My brother has a giant one almost 5 feet long of 1⅛-inch steel for really big jobs.

A simple bar, but just as useful, is a straight one with a chisel tip that is flat on one side and angled on the other, for prying. I use two of these a lot in stonework. One is 3 feet long, of ¾-inch round spring steel, and the other is 1¼-inch square stock, 5½ feet long. The big one is medium carbon, about like axle steel, and is quenched only. It's handy for dig-

This froe is not hand forged, being one my grandfather bought many years ago. It's drop-forged, a factory process in which the heated steel is stamped to shape under power in a die.

SPLIT WITH HOT CHISEL

WRECKING BAR

CHISEL POINT

-SPRING STEEL-

My brother John's bigger wrecking bar, forged of 1⅛-inch steel, 4 feet long, for obstinate jobs.

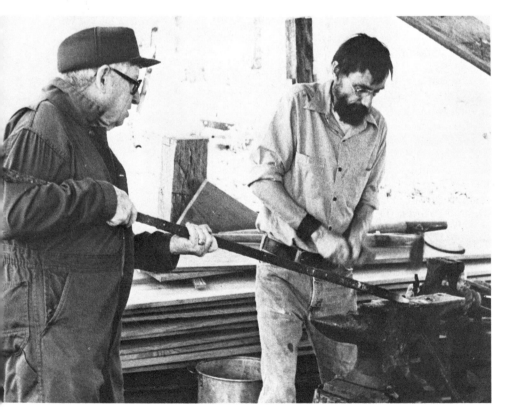

Hammering the chisel point on a heavy digging bar of 1⅛-inch steel. After the initial shaping is done, we switch to the anvil horn to avoid denting the face with the edge of the hammer. This medium-carbon steel is quenched only, from cherry-red heat to produce a tough but not brittle edge without drawing the temper.

ging or prying stones out of the ground, lifting whole buildings or mired trucks.

If you're attempting a hand-dug well or septic tank, this big digging bar is good to use instead of a pick, for which there is often no room to swing. The bar has enough mass to shatter pretty big rocks that are in your way.

Since automotive axles are too short for a good digging bar, look in junkyards for old shafting, which usually has about the same carbon content. This is tough steel, as opposed to hard steel, and is good for high-impact uses. A favorite in the old days was Model T Ford drive shafting. Old mills often had line shafting overhead, from which pulleys and belts drove machinery, and this in varying sizes can still be found. I have a pile of square reinforcing bar from a 1920s overpass recently demolished, which seems to be uniformly usable. Modern re-bar hasn't proven reliable.

For any sort of logwork, you'll need a cant hook, or two if you have help. These are usually cheap at junkshops just now, but are so simple to make we'll discuss it. The band is mild steel, about ¼ inch by 2 inches, punched and drifted for about a ½-inch pin. The hook should be at least medium carbon, and the length varies. I use a small hook, 12 inches or so, for most cabin logs, and logs for beams and joists. Then I have a larger one of 18 inches or so for the big stuff. Often two of us will handle a log, with the big hook on the butt end and the small one at the other.

The iron parts of a cant hook for handling logs. The hook is shaft steel flattened to ½-inch thickness, tempered for toughness, to a straw color. The handle strap is old wagon tire.

A finished cant hook.

109

Hook stock can be coil spring steel, sheared heavy spring leaf of at least ⅜-inch thickness, or small shafting. I usually start with coil of ¾-inch thickness and hammer it flat to from ⅜ inch to ½ inch thick. Upset some metal at the hook angle for more strength, and hammer a 3-inch point. Quench and temper to purple or blue.

Pin with a tough steel pin or hardened bolt, since wear will make the hook floppy, and you want this tool to bite every time. Often a cant hook's slipping will put several hundred pounds of log onto your body, sometimes from up on raised skid poles, and that hurts.

Another band for the end of the handle is a good idea, to keep the wood from slipping and eventually splitting. I like to punch a hole in both the hook band and the end band for a screw to help hold it in place. Put both bands on hot so they'll be tight when they cool, but don't burn the wood.

The handle gets a lot of strain, and should be at least 3 inches in diameter at the hook band. Somehow, these handles are prohibitively expensive in hardware stores, although symmetrical and presumably easier to make than axe handles and such. I usually use 3-inch-square shagbark hickory for cant hook handles, sawn at the local sawmill and seasoned for several years.

Most of your carpentry tools are better bought secondhand at sales and flea markets than made by hand. Handsaws and squares and folding rules are not expensive, as are the heavier tools for basic structural work. Your forge can supply you with all the tools the early settlers used, and these will let you build structures similar to theirs. For finished carpentry and masonry you could tackle making your own tools, but we approach a point of diminishing returns here that's too significant to ignore.

CHAPTER EIGHT

House Hardware

Blacksmithing for your homestead needs makes a lot of sense when you consider that all the necessary ironwork for house and farm came from the smithy up until 150 years ago. There were cast metal items from the foundry, too, but these were rare in the new settlements. Most of the hinges, latches, hooks, chain, nails, and even the tools were recycled from old horseshoes, wagon tires, and other worn iron.

Certainly you can buy everything you need for cabin, toolshed, and barn today, but let's carry your preferred personal statement, the hand-built house, on into hand-forged hardware. Look at your living room (perhaps your only room): front door strap hinges and latch of your own design, window hardware; the complete fireplace set of andirons, swinging crane, bellows, cooking grate, poker, shovel, tongs, and broom with perhaps a stand for these; hammered wall sconces for candles, or holders for kerosene lamps, ceiling lighting fixtures that may be for electricity or flame. Coat hooks. The forged iron straps that support your ceiling joists from kingposts above.

And the kitchen. Here's a room that will keep your forge going for weeks. The pot rack, in any one of its interpretations, is a major project. We tried a circular hanging one, which holds lots of pots, but it didn't fit with the shape of our kitchen. The present one is three successive bars out from the wall with double hooks. The circular one, which is easier, I make regularly, sometimes with a heavy forged hook out from the wall to hang it from. We'll discuss making this one later.

In forged household hardware, the principle of unity, or working from one piece of iron, is most important. Here your work is not just useful, it's also on constant display. A fireplace crane can be a vertical piece swiveling from eyes set into masonry, attached to a horizontal piece with a hook, all braced with an angle piece. But it's more aesthetic if the entire swinging part is one piece, with perhaps the brace curved down to the wall and the hook integral. This could be welded, riveted, or joined with

Wayne Haymes and I hammer a 36-inch strap hinge at his shop in Hollister, Missouri, using the 8-pound hammer.

a loop-and-eye, but the one-piece is stronger, more graceful, and most important here, it looks better. We'll discuss forging one of these later, too.

I occasionally hammer a candle holder complete with handle from a single bar of iron. Sheet iron would be simpler, with the handle riveted in, but the grace of the single piece, and the evidence of more handwork, are pleasing.

In our kitchen we use a lot of black cast-ironware, and we hang them on individual one-piece hooks driven into overhead beams. Similar hooks with holes punched can be mounted with forged nails, or screws into the studwall if you lack beams.

My own approach to house hardware is utilitarian. Ornamentation is usually whatever I've seen and adapted, or a simple twist or curl that seems logical. Hinges (for instance for kitchen cabinets or front door) I prefer as strap-and-pintle instead of double-strap. I notice this a lot in New England forgework, too. The pintle is simple, largely unseen, and strong, being a one-piece pin and mounting. Ornamentation goes into the strap. Of course, the original and still valid purpose of the strap of a hinge was to span and bind the several boards of the door. Long straps still give a look of strength, whether it's needed or not.

While we're on the subject, fake straps are a waste of time. The honesty of forged metal demands usefulness. We have a sliding closet door in our loft bathroom (no room to swing a door) with forge hardware. The pull handle is a simple loop, but it becomes a strap bracing the three 1-inch by 12-inch boards of the door. I had in mind a spade ornament at the end, but tried a leaf instead. Subsequently forged leaves began to appear throughout the house, which seems to fit with our near-wilderness location.

A couple we know live really far back in the woods in a frame house. They've undertaken to replace everything in it with handmade things, from leaded glass windows and copper lamps and handmade woodstoves to all the furniture and even kitchen utensils. I hammered a set of carbon steel carving knives for them in trade for copperwork.

That may be going a bit far for most of us, but certainly the feeling of self-sufficiency increases with the number of handmade pieces in use. Cup hooks, plant hanging hooks, towel racks, mirror frames, and

Sliding linen-closet door pull and bathroom paper holder in our log house, both with hammered, veined leaf design.

Forged paper towel rack, to hold turned spindle.

plain forged nails driven into log walls to hang things from, all are simple, useful items from your shop. The barn board bed we sleep on is braced with forged pieces at the corners. So is the table we eat on. And shelves can be put up with those tin braces from the store, but your forged brackets look better and hold more weight.

Essentially, any metal piece in your house can be made by hand if you have the skill, material, and time. The obvious dividing line for you is the time investment you want to make for the sake of forged hardware. I use a lot of forged nails and brackets, but buy the screws. If something looks good and works with rivets, I don't buy bolts for it unless I'm pressed for time. I have made bolts, and sometimes still do, but except for rare uses, they can be had cheaper recycled or from the hardware store.

In our own house, I began replacing hinges and other pieces we'd bought in the hurry of building, with forged work. Once the new pieces began to take shape under my hammer, I could see design possibilities, and I let the work grow as it would.

I am always impressed by the craftsmanship of a really great ornamental ironsmith such as the late Samuel Yellin, and some of the young artists in Dona Meilach's book *Decorative and Sculptural Ironwork.** Few of us homestead smiths will attain that level of excellence, and that's not the direction my own work takes. I will always rather forge a drawknife or a mill pick than a chandelier. But I will do simple ornamental work, letting the decoration follow the function of the piece.

Your own house may become filled with artful iron, and I hope it does, but let it all have its uses. Utility is most important, but there is room for art in useful iron.

*Dona Z. Meilach, *Decorative and Sculptural Ironwork* (New York: Crown Publishers, 1977).

FIREPLACE CRANE

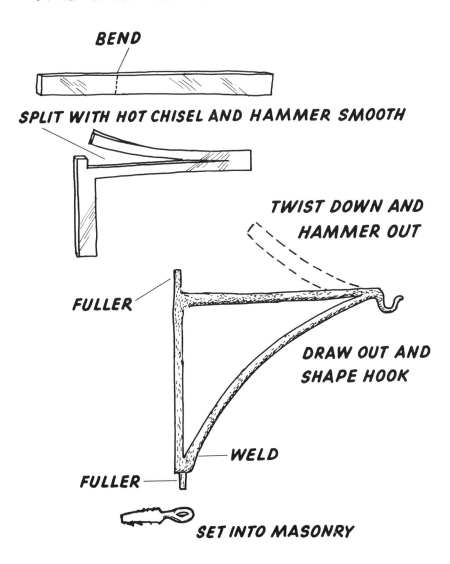

BEND

SPLIT WITH HOT CHISEL AND HAMMER SMOOTH

TWIST DOWN AND
HAMMER OUT

FULLER

DRAW OUT AND
SHAPE HOOK

WELD

FULLER

SET INTO MASONRY

We mentioned the fireplace crane earlier, so let's go into some detail on this project. We'll do it one-piece. The size is up to you, depending, of course, on the size of the fireplace. It's a good idea to anchor the crane in the masonry of the side wall, making it long enough to reach to the center of the fire. By pivoting the crane from near the front of the side wall, you can swing the crane back pretty much out of the way, and bring it out away from the fire for fine touches during cooking.

Say we have an 18-inch crane, 12 inches high. We'll use a piece of ⅜-inch by 2-inch bar stock about 24 inches long. Heat and reheat as necessary. First bend a 90-degree corner in it about 8 inches from one end (the bottom) over the edge of the anvil. It doesn't matter if you square the outside of the bend, but it will be neater if you do. So upset toward the corner as you bend.

Now, use the hot cut ¾ inch from the corner to make a cut down from the top to halfway through the horizontal, long leg of the bar. Turn the hot cut at right angles and split the bar down the center to maybe 4 inches from the end. Bend this cut bar out and draw it from its nearly 12-inch length to about 18 inches long, smoothing the cut edge as you do.

Smooth the edge of the other half of the horizontal bar, too, but don't draw it. Now twist this bar so that the longer, thinner half is under it, and hammer the twist out. This will lengthen the bar a bit, but not much.

Now draw the end where both bars are still joined, out to a long point. Bend down into a hook for the pots to hang on, with maybe a little reverse lip at the tip.

The vertical leg can now be drawn to near its 12-inch height. Scarf the end of both this and of the long, thin bar you bent down. Curve this bar to come against the vertical with a bit of pressure to hold it as you weld it. If the curved bar is too long, cut some off; if too short, draw it some more.

Heat, flux, heat, and weld this joint. You'll probably bend the brace bar in the process, but you can get the curve back later. Now fuller or hammer a narrow neck, in the end of the welded joint for a rounded protrusion 1 inch long with a substantial shoulder. If you don't have swages, just roll the fullered end as you hammer at the edge of the anvil. The shoulder will be for the mounting eye. Round the corner you left sticking up on top, too, for the other eye, but draw this one out about ¾ inch farther.

Now hammer loops in two round rods of at least ⅜ inch diameter, 6 inches or so long, Bend a 90-degree angle in each near the other end. You can weld the loops if you like, but it isn't necessary. And you can get a better circle if you don't, probably.

Now, if your fireplace is already built, we'll have to dig out some mortar between stones or bricks to set the eyes in place. Figure your

One of my favorite fireplace poker ends is begun by drawing out a piece of ⅜-inch or ½-inch round stock, then bending it over . . .

. . . so that the point is laid back onto the shank. Then the joint is fluxed, heated and forge welded . . .

. . . and the final point and barb are hammered. The other end may be a loop, basket, or knob.

height to come out right beforehand, since it's harder to drill stone or brick than the mortar between them. Dig out enough to allow the eyes at least 3 inches of depth, then push them in and mortar again, keeping it damp for several days to cure.

Now slip the longer upper pintle of the crane up through the eye far enough to let the bottom one clear and drop back in. There should still be plenty of the top pintle to hold. If there isn't, you can work on both the top and bottom ones to get them right.

You may not be able to get a clean cut at the end where the two bars join. By using the hot cut flat on the anvil you can cut almost to the end faster, but you get a tapered cut. Switch to another technique for the last half inch or so. Heat, then clamp the iron in the vise and drive the chisel down from the end for a cleaner end cut.

If there are still rough places when you're finished, file them. I always heat again to black heat and quench in oil to get rid of shiny file marks. As a last step, unless I plan to paint the piece, I give it all the blacksmith's oil finish at black heat. You won't want to paint the crane, because the fire will burn it all off.

Of course it would be easier to start with three bars of iron and weld up the crane than to do it from one piece. It would also be easier to arc weld the pieces, but we're talking about blacksmithing here, not the coldwork you can find in any hardware store selling ornamental iron.

We've mentioned hinges, and you'll need a bit of practice to get them right. I don't like to try to copy commercial hardware, with two or three loops around the pin. I form a single loop around a pintle, gate-style. When figuring the length of iron to allow for the loop, there's a bit more to it than pi (or 3.14) times the diameter of the pin. What happens when you make the loop is that the outside metal stretches, as you'd expect, but the inside of the loop upsets, to leave you with too little metal. There are several formulas different smiths I know use. One of these formulas works fairly well: Pi times pin diameter plus half the pin diameter again.

I will admit to never measuring iron for a loop. I just hammer whatever iron I need to get around a forming pin of the right size, then draw the hinge strap to the right length. If the hinge is to be a matched, strap-and-strap one, I loop first, then cut out what I don't want with a hacksaw. That's for a one-and-one loop, a two-and-one loop, or a two-and-two loop hinge with both straps even.

Drawing and tapering the strap, which is the usual treatment, will give you thicker iron near the point, unless you keep hammering it thin. This stretches the iron a lot, so you can easily get half again the length of the bar you started with. If you cut into the bar for ornamentation along the strap, you can get a taper of sorts with little drawing.

The ornamentation at the end of the hinge strap is as hard a pro-

CUT OUT

HINGE PIN CUTOUT

PINTLES

ject as you want to make it. A simple flattened circle is common and is a basic example of uncluttered design. These were usually done from just the metal at the end of the strap, so were quite thin, stepping down from the strap thickness. I usually upset, or leave more iron when I taper, so I can do the circle full thickness. Form the circle while the iron is still thick, or it'll fold too easily. Then flatten after you have the basic circle.

The spade is just a pointed circle. Both these should have a clean shoulder, done on the edge of the anvil or with a shouldering tool. This tool can be just a blunt cold chisel. Do the point of the spade on the horn for the reverse curve.

The double curve and the fleur-de-lis are accomplished by splitting the iron with the hot cut, then bending the points to one side for room to work them. This is close work, and like most ornamental iron-

Wayne Haymes at work on a large strap hinge. Wayne did commercial blacksmithing in Hollister, Missouri.

The hinge pin being riveted with the ball peen hammer for a decorative effect.

120

Artist Chandis Ingenthron, who's worked with me on several books, gets into the smithy now and then. Here he's forged a double wall hook, with fleur-de-lis ornamentation. The flat surfaces of the hook were decorated with a design done cold with the center punch.

work, it takes patience and a light touch. I get a good idea of a student's control on a pair of fleur-de-lis strap hinges. Be prepared for almost instant heating of this delicate iron in the forge. It's easy to burn it, and the heat goes away quickly from these small masses of metal, too. Much of the final shaping can actually be done cold if you're careful, and haven't picked up carbon steel by mistake.

When making hinge sets, it's a good idea to alternate operations so you can keep them matched better. It's hard to remember how much iron you cut for a curl after it's drawn and finished. By doing one step at a time to each of the hinges, you'll get a better-looking pair or set.

If you rivet halves of a strap-and-strap hinge, it'll almost always be too tight, like the tongs you made. Heat the joint to a medium red, then work the hinge until it cools. And oil it, or it'll tighten up again.

Your household ironware should have a finish of character. It doesn't matter how a cold chisel looks if it cuts iron, but you'll want the iron that's on view to look right. Don't try for that fakey rippled effect that's supposed to look like hammering. A rule of mine is that every bit of the surface of a piece of ornamental iron should be hammered. And I don't try for a particularly smooth or a particularly rough finish, I just let it work out. It looks hand forged because it is.

A potrack of some sort is almost a kitchen necessity, and I seem to

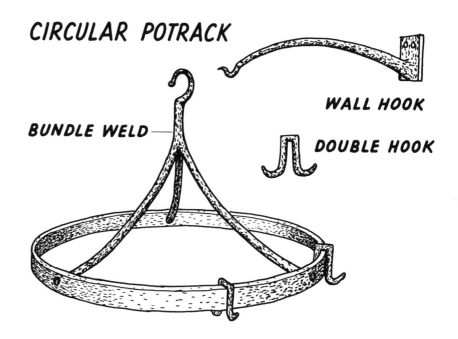

CIRCULAR POTRACK

WALL HOOK

BUNDLE WELD

DOUBLE HOOK

Potrack to hang over kitchen butcher block. The square is ½-inch-by-3-inch steel, riveted at the corners to angle iron for the loop-and-bar chain. The pothooks are single, split double, and bundle-welded triple.

The basket twist is made by forge welding several rods together at each end. Then the bundle is heated in the center and twisted in the vise.

Reversing the twist in the bundle-welded piece makes each rod stand out.

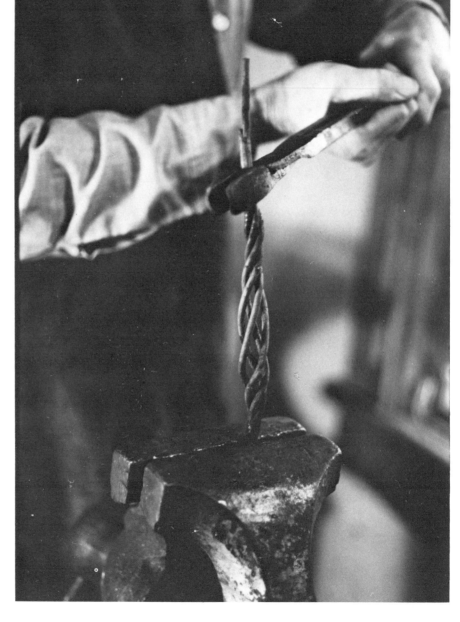

make potracks often. The most accessible is a circular one, to be hung from overhead or suspended from a heavy hook out from the wall.

I use ¼-inch-by-2-inch stock for a hoop about 24 inches in diameter. A smaller rack of 16 inches or so needs to be about 1 inch or 1½ inch strap. Figure the length as simple pi times the diameter. Heat and bend on the anvil horn to form the hoop, correcting the arc as needed. Scarf the ends, and spring them together for a firm fit when welding. Flux when red hot, then bring to welding heat. Have the anvil horn close to make the weld on.

Now, you'll want three holes in the hoop, so you can strengthen your weld joint by punching one through its lap if you like (you'll be riveting a spoke through here). I use ¼-inch or ⅜-inch rod for spokes in the hoop, so punch the three holes the right size at equal distances around. You'll distort the circle somewhat in doing this, but it's easy to reshape.

Bunch the three spokes, with one extending about an inch longer, past the joint to be welded. Wrap the bundle with wire to hold it together. Now flux, heat, and weld, turning the bundle rapidly as you hammer it. Shape the weld, then draw the extra inch of rod and form a hook.

The length of these spokes is up to you, depending on how low you want the hoop to hang. I use a length 1½ times the hoop radius (one will be that 1 inch longer), and curve each spoke upward to the weld. You can curve the spokes before welding, but it's hard to hold them in line if you do. Shape them by eye, or draw out a curve on paper to match them against.

Put each spoke end through its hole in the hoop, heat, and rivet, with the spoke held in the vise. If the whole thing is lopsided when you're through, you can heat and bend one way or another to straighten it.

The pothooks I usually make are double, and are hung over the hoop, as many as seems right. I use ¼-inch rod about 5 inches long, drawing both ends to a point. Then I bend in the center, making a long staple. Heat the tips, and start both the hook bends at the same time on the anvil horn. You can work the hooks for a tight fit on the hoop or leave them loose.

And you can file round notches in the hoop with a chainsaw file if you want the hooks to stay in place. Or even punch more holes and put the hooks through. My wife likes to be able to move the hooks for more or less room, so I just leave them mobile.

I got the idea for this potrack from a unique wheelbarrow wheel a man once showed me. He made a riddle of it, asking if I'd ever seen a functioning wheel without an axle. Or even a spindle. Well, no, I guessed I hadn't. So he produced this hoop, with three alternating spokes on each side, curved out from the rim, welded and shaped into two shafts. A neat job, and one you may want to try.

It means simply six spokes, with the odd ones joining at one side or the other. Care must be taken to get the wheel balanced, or it'll wobble easily. I would definitely rivet one spoke through the lapweld, since trundling the wheelbarrow around over rocks might eventually break it apart here.

The number of household goodies you can forge is limitless. I like to make as much of the house hardware as possible, coordinating the design. So spade hinges might repeat a spade mounting bracket on a towel rack. Or spade ends on door handles and drawer pulls.

Our own design is a leaf of indeterminate species, which appears throughout the house. Hammering the leaf is a simple job, but it can be made fancy. The basic shape is just an elongated spade. The veins of the leaf are cut with a chisel while the leaf is straight (the veins are actually carved on the surface); then if you want a curl, the straight lines curl along with the leaf. You could serrate the edges of the leaf with a three-cornered file for an elm-leaf look, but that'd leave you with sharp edges, which you might not want.

Advanced ornamental ironwork, such as grape clusters with leaves and tendrils, will require a lot of practice and take a lot of time to execute. You'll use all the techniques of ironworking to produce the intri-

Veining leaves can be done cold as shown. Then, when heated and curled, the veining curls with the shape of the leaf.

Leaf design on strap hinge on tongue-in-groove cedar door.

Another leaf design hinge and the ¼″ by 1″ strap both halves were made of.

Riveting the square tenon of a hook for a paper towel spindle, onto the leaf-design mounting bracket. Such riveting can be done cold for a tighter joint, or tightened later, since the heated tenon contracts when cold.

cate detail of this kind of work. If this is to become your specialty, try to find another smith who does decorative work, to learn from.

Remember a simple basic in your houseware forging: Function dictates the general appearance of the piece. A door handle may be as ornamental as a piece of baroque furniture, but the handle must still open that door. I favor primitive blacksmithing, which is practically all function.

Forging a Set of Andirons

(opposite, left)

A pair of andirons begins with splitting a recycled bar of ½-inch-by-2-inch mild steel with the hot chisel. Each step was duplicated with the matching piece, for better comparison and closer similarity.

(upper right)

One bar is spread over the anvil horn while the other heats in the forge.

The rough edges of the cut are smoothed, and the feet are formed.

Feet are flattened and finished. The hammer used is my favorite, a 3-pound, 45-degree-peen, hand-forged one.

The stem of the upright half of the andiron is tapered, leaving metal near the "Y" for the horizontal half, and at the end for the ornamental ball.

Metal at the end of the upright is folded over preparatory to forge welding (called a faggot weld) to thicken for shaping a ball.

Borax flux is sprinkled on the joint at low red heat.

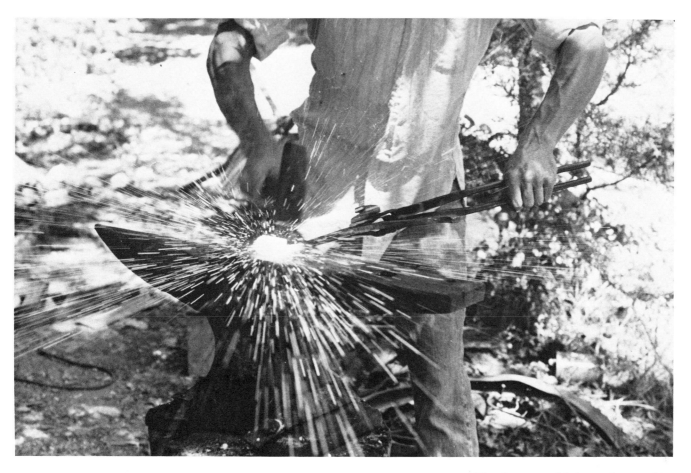

The faggot weld is made at white heat, with a minimum of pounding, to retain thickness. Sparks are droplets of molten metal and bits of scale.

(upper left)
The welded end is shaped while still hot into a crude, elongated ball.

(upper right)
The ball is finished with a light hammer.

(lower left)
The upright is heated and punched with a square punch. A hot punch with a handle could be used here, to keep hands away from the hot metal.

(lower right)
The hole, started from the other side, is finished by turning over and punching on through over first the pritchel hole, then the hardy hole as it is spread larger.

The horizontal bar of the andiron is shaped at the end into a tenon, to fit the punched hole in the upright.

Final shaping of the tenon is done with a file for an exact fit.

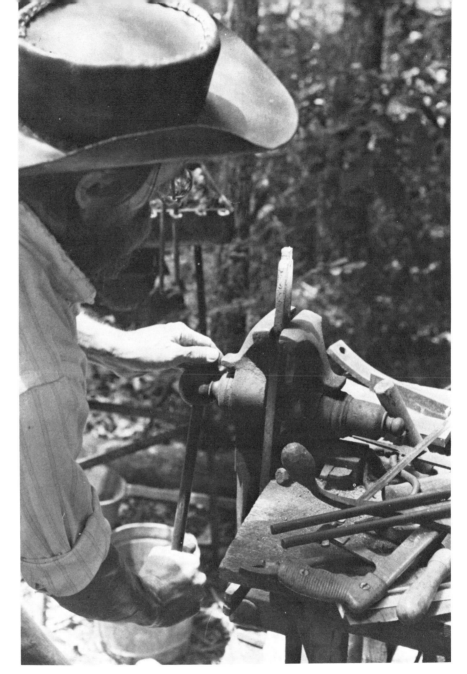

The heated tenon end is clamped into the vise.

133

The two halves of the andiron are riveted together with the ball peen. As the joint cools, it will loosen with contraction, so both pieces may be heated, or the riveted joint reheated and tightened.

The riveted joint.

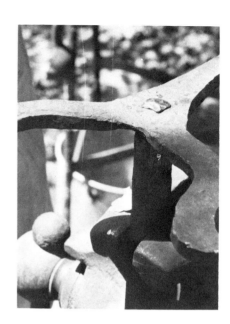

The complete andirons. This set was a custom-made gift for the Virgil Culler family of Bethel, Missouri, for the fireplace I built for them in the hewn log house they built with my assistance.

CHAPTER NINE

Homestead Tools and Repairs

Your specific pursuits around your farmstead will determine how much your blacksmithing will help things along. If you plan a nearly self-sufficient operation, the uses of the forge are limitless. I have forged braces for a water wheel, brackets for a windmill, pieces for a sawmill, and may one day build a steam engine. The forge is a lot of help in the power-independence game. Certain needs and activities are common to most of us backwoods dwellers, and we'll talk about a few here.

A great deal of your time in wilderness living will be spent moving things around: large things like stones, logs, lumber, firewood, gravel, sand, and other building materials. A pickup truck is handy; if you live in rough country a four-wheel-drive one is better. But there are jobs for which this workhorse just isn't suited, such as moving long logs or boards, or hauling stones too heavy to lift, or work in terrain too rough to build a road in. And you may not be able to justify the cost, either.

Two conveyances have been around farms for centuries, and they're still indispensable: the sled (sledge), and the cart or two-wheeled trailer. Both can be fashioned with the help of your forge and some wood, and with an axle and wheels for the trailer.

Let's look at the sled first. It can be as little as 6 inches off the ground and still clear most obstacles, and its low profile means you tumble stones, firewood blocks, or logs onto it without lifting. Its oak runners are quickly shod with two steel spring leaves, and a floor of 1-inch or 2-inch oak laid across the top. Hooks or loops for the pull chain should be bolted to the runners themselves, since that's where the resistance comes from.

Heat the spring leaf runner steel and hammer it flat, then give it a curve upward in front to fit your shaped runners. Now heat the steel, punch and drift out at least three tapered holes with a large center punch. This taper is to countersink big flat-head screws that hold the steel in place. Use the tie-bolt hole in the leaf for one of the holes.

A castoff aluminum pulley becomes a sheave for use on a lifting boom.

The sled will last longer if, after you deck it, you turn it upside down and bolt in angle braces fore and aft holding runner to deck. Some ⅜-inch by 2-inch steel is heavy enough, each piece about 5 inches long, and it'll keep the runners vertical. They get loose otherwise as you skid around rocks and stumps, pulled by faithful mule, tractor, 4wd, or your own muscle.

One bit of caution in using a steel-runner sled: It can run into, over, or under whatever's pulling it if your're headed downhill with a load. A pull device similar to an automotive towbar would take care of the problem with tractor or vehicle: your mule would need shafts and a complete set of buggy harness.

I have an old set of sled pull-hooks I picked up, forged from a wagon tire, that are designed to keep the chain from coming loose. The hooks curve back a long way, with a bend inward at the tip. The crossbar hook common in New England is another good idea here. The old-timers never had enough chain just to leave the piece on the sled when not in use; it was forever being borrowed for some other use.

The two-wheeled trailer is somewhat more complicated. A farm cart could have just about anything for wheels and bearings, but you'll use yours for highway travel, so plan to use an automotive axle, wheels, and springs. I've put together a few with no springs, but jarring under a load will eventually crack or break important parts when you need the trailer most—like when you have a load of sacked cement with rain approaching and no tarpaulin.

I prefer a conventional junkyard I-beam front axle from a pickup truck or pre-coil spring car. A rear axle is heavier, which is sometimes better, depending on what you plan to haul. The dropped front axle usually allows a lower trailer. With it, I forge a clamp to hold the tie rod, keeping the wheels straight ahead. You can also weld them straight, but that makes it harder to recycle the axle later.

If you have steel for framing, fine. Heavy-angle iron, at least 4 inches wide and ⅜ inch thick, or channel iron is good. If these are not available, a good frame is oak 2 by 8 timbers or even 2 by 6's. At this writing, I'm helping my neighbor build one with such a frame. I forged a set of spring shackles, the flat bars that hold a pin through the leaf spring end loops, and put ½-inch holes in them, then we bored larger holes in the wood, lined with ½-inch water pipe bushings for the swing shackle bolts. The stationary shackles were bolted solidly to the wood. You may be able to find an axle with U-bolts, springs, and shackles attached.

We reinforced the 2-inch framing at the corners with heavy-angle iron, which I forged. It was 4 inches high and bolted with four bolts at each corner for stability. Another cross member was angle-iron braced across the center to support the tongue, which was also angle braced.

Diagonal bracing helped reinforce the tapered, 2 by 6 oak tongue.

FARM SLED

SPIKES — OAK FLOOR

2X6 OAK RUNNERS

FORGED ANGLE BRACES AT LEAST 3/8"X I"

PULL-CHAIN HOOK

USE LARGE CENTER PUNCH

COUNTERSINK HOLES FOR LARGE FLAT HEAD SCREWS

HAMMER
SPRING LEAF TO RUNNER CURVE, NORMALIZE

TWO WHEELED CART OR FARM TRAILER

2 X 8 OAK

FRONT AUTOMOTIVE AXLE

HOLE WITH BUSHING

RIGID FRONT SHACKLE

HARDENED BOLTS

BOLTED CLAMP FOR HOLDING TIE ROD RIGID

AXLE

TIE ROD

AXLE BACK OF CENTER

2"X8" OAK FRAME

TONGUE

ANGLE BRACES

LAG SCREWS

TONGUE

FLOORING

FRAME

TAPERED 2"X6" TONGUE

FORGED BRACES

LOOPS FOR TYING THINGS DOWN

FORGED SIDEWALL BRACES

FENDER BRACES

Forged farm trailer braces, at the hinged tailgate. Harness rings were added at the tops of the braces to tie things to. The wood was painted with oil sealer and red barn paint, the iron with flat black.

An unbraced wooden trailer tongue can snap off if you jackknife it while backing or if you accidentally drop your anvil on it.

Decking this trailer with 1-inch oak was simple, since it was all done between the wheels. My own farm trailer, with heavier axle, frame, wheels, and springs, extends out to enclose the wheels in boxes. Forged braces hold on sides as needed, and my tailgate and front wall are mounted on hinges for extra length when dropped.

Now, I have often been in a location, or in a state of penury, that precluded a store-bought trailer hitch and ball. My Land-Rover uses a heavy pin, so my current trailer has no ball hitch, but I've forged several, and if you want to tackle it, here's how:

First you need a ball. When I get a blacksmithing student who needs a challenge, I have him hammer out a trailer ball from one piece of truck axle shaft. It takes a lot of time, so you'll want to buy one, I'm sure. To fit the hitch, I clamp the ball in the vise and wrap a 24-inch piece of 2½-inch-by-¼-inch mild steel around it, cupping it front and sides on top, and at the front on the bottom. Work it till it will drop over the ball nicely, then fit snugly as you pull the bottom lip back under it.

TRAILER HITCH

START WITH 24" STRAP 1/4" X 2"
BEND AND SHAPE AROUND
BALL IN VISE

TONGUE

SAFETY
CHAIN

This sturdy trailer hitch reaches far up under today's tin cars to attach to heavier framework. It's made of heavy angle and bar stock, forged, and arc welded.

Now punch holes for mounting on the tongue, one for a safety chain, and another pair of pivot bolt holes for the fork that will hold everything in place. This fork should be forged to fit the ball, with a loop around the pivot bolt. I make a square hole in the fork for a heavy carriage bolt to draw it up into place. This bolt goes up through a ¼-inch plate that can extend from the tongue as a separate piece or be welded to the hitch. I use a nut with a loop in it for safety wire so the nut won't unscrew until I'm ready for it to. Or you can thread a hole punched in a bar shaped to the purpose.

Several of these homemade hitches are running around the country on trailers I've made, and have given good service. As I said, though, you'd save by buying one already made and putting your expertise to work elsewhere.

If you put permanent sides on your trailer, do reinforce the corners with bolted angle braces. The vibration from country non-roads will soon loosen the tightest screw or nail, even in tough wood. And forge some loops and hooks along the sides for tying things in place.

I like to paint the ironwork black on a wooden trailer, no matter what color the wood is. And do keep your trailer or sled inside when not in use. In my part of the country most of these useful contrivances rust or rot away in a few years when they could last generations.

Your 4wd or pickup truck will probably have a bumper hitch already, but you may want to fabricate one for your car. Most post-1960 cars are unit-body, which means they're made of tin and not much else, so a strong hitch is a problem. I bolt bracing for steel to whatever looks solid, and use a broad washer or piece of plate around the bolt to distribute the stress over as much tin as possible. It's important to brace for up-and-down thrust as well as straight-forward pull and side-to-side pull.

I've just fashioned a hitch for our Volvo station wagon. It's meant reaching far under for something solid to tie to, past the exhaust pipe and gas tank. I gave the hitch longitudinal stability with two ¼-inch by 1½-inch bars, on edge, bolted to heavy ridges up near the rear axle. Vertical bracing came down from the 3-bolt bumper mounting plate at each side. Heavy angle iron went across to mount the hitch on, which was a piece ½-inch by 2½-inches, extended back. Then ½-inch square bars are angled from the ends of this piece to as near the bumper mount as possible to take much of the stress from the angle iron. It is a tough hitch.

Let's get on to the useful tools around your farm or woods retreat. A tool you'll be forever grateful for discovering is the splitting maul. And it's become quite expensive, with the return to wood heat. As my blacksmith friend Wayne Haymes says, "If you want simplicity in this life, you've got to be willing to pay for it."

Here's what I've done repeatedly for self, friends, and customers:

My 8-pound splitting maul, forged from a junkyard sledgehammer head. The handle is drawknifed of shagbark hickory, and has lasted many seasons.

Buy a chipped head of a sledgehammer of about 8 pounds at a junkshop or sale (never pay more than a dollar for the head), and forge a maul from it. It pays to have help here, though I've done it alone with the short-handled 6-pound hammer I use. Beating on 8 pounds of carbon steel with anything less is a waste. Watch for folding as you taper the edge. I put a bit of reverse curve in on the anvil horn, and hammer the final edge to the desired sharpness (but don't make it too sharp). Quench and temper draw to a purple; you'll want to use the hammer face to drive wedges with and don't want the face to chip. I've had my share of flying bits of steel from factory tools that were left too hard.

Don't try punching a handle hole in a 3-inch block of steel to forge a maul from stock. It's just too much work. If you make the maul or hammer this way, start your hole small and work up.

Splitting wedges are easy to forge from large-diameter shafting, 2 or 3 inches. Try the finished product for hardness after quenching; you shouldn't need to draw the temper, since most shafting is medium carbon. If you do, temper draw from the hammer end. When this end mushrooms with use, heat and forge back into shape, or trim off the overhang. Again a misplaced blow could send hardened steel flying.

This toothed rock chisel is cherry red and ready to quench. Temper will be drawn to straw at the points. Teeth were ground and filed while the piece was annealed.

A cold chisel is among the first things I have a student make. Shearing rusty boltheads, splitting rusty nuts, cutting bars, and rivetheads—any cold cutting requires a good chisel. And a good chisel is one that's long enough that you don't hit your thumb, your knuckle, or skin your hand on when the rusty steel you're cutting gives way. Too much live bark has been knocked off with those cute little toys you buy in their raised plastic-covered cards.

I use a bar of carbon steel, 100-point or so (coil spring or star drill shank) ¾ to 1 inch in diameter, and at least 8 inches long. That much mass means you have to use a bigger hammer, but it's worth it to keep down the tetanus. Draw to a long taper, then shape the edge much more blunt, a sixty-to-ninety-degree angle. A keen edge will work on softer metals, but if it's hard enough to cut, it will eventually break or chip.

Sharpen while annealed, then heat and quench. Draw from the hammer end to a straw if spring steel, to purple if higher carbon. Experiment; you may want a harder or softer temper for your own uses.

I usually taper the heads of punches, chisels, and wedges to lessen mushrooming. This will also keep the impact path nearer the center and lessen the chances of bending if you really get on the tool with a sledgehammer.

Making a Cold Chisel

To forge a cold chisel, first a section of automotive coil spring is heated in the forge and straightened in the vise.

An eight-inch piece is cut off on the hardy.

(upper left)
And straightened further.

(upper right)
Then the steel is heated and the tapered cutting edge hammered.

(lower right)
The struck end is tapered and trued up in the vise.

146

(upper left)

The chisel is annealed by cooling slowly from cherry red, either in ashes or sand, or as shown here, next to the forge fire while other work is going on.

(upper right)

While softened by annealing, the chisel is ground to an edge, and any rough places smoothed, cold.

(lower left)

The working part of the finished chisel is heated to cherry red and quenched to harden.

(lower right)

The chisel is honed or ground to a shiny surface so the tempering colors can be seen. Then it is laid on a low forge fire so that colors will run toward the cutting edge. This will leave the rest of the tool normalized, so as not to be brittle, but the edge hardest. A bronze at the edge is right for most work, using this 95 point steel.

For woods living the cant hook we talked about earlier is a big help. I was raised around a sawmill and used one from early on. If you plan to do much with logs in their round state, have a hook or hooks that bite properly. And have some help around, too; about all you can say for the behavior of logs and other large masses is that they barely tolerate you.

Log grabhooks are good if properly made. Bad ones waste time as you back your tractor, mule, or 4wd to rehook after they've pulled out. Two simple hooks on a ring won't do much. A scissors action is better, since the forward pull clamps the hooks tighter. But point angle and sharpness have a lot to do with whether grabhooks save or waste time. My best advice here is to experiment with your own pair if you plan to skid many logs. The hook is made the same way as the cant hook, but of heavier stock, about an inch thick.

Often I use a loop in a chain to skid logs, being mindful of the time I caught my thumb in one as the skidding tractor lurched forward. That was a dancing exhibition, with my peacock-blue thumbnail afire.

Sharpening plow points used to be a standard job for country blacksmiths. It's a lot like drawing a blunt axe head. You're thinning the remaining metal to get a sharp point, then hardening and retempering. Often you'll weld new carbon steel onto the old, as with the axe. It's a valid exercise for both axe and plow point if the replacement is too difficult, although as I mentioned earlier, a new point can often be forged as quickly.

My brother and I used an old Oliver 20 sulky plow for years, and the flintrock on his farm dulled or broke several points. We were lucky to find points in junkshops and flea markets here and there for a while, but did in time use up the region's supply. I had resolved to forge the next one we needed from a grader blade cutting edge, but the occasion never came up. We may have hit the last rock in his fields, though I doubt it. Anyway, the plow reposes, replaced now, with a good point still on it.

The forge can be the saving of antique tools and equipment like that old plow. I have replaced many missing parts on my Model A pickup truck with hand-forged work, from spring shackles to bumpers. When your fondness runs to exotic or ancient machinery or both, your skills with iron will be tried. You don't find a crank or a drawbar brace for a fifty-year-old tractor at the local parts store, so you make such a crank or brace. And the disc harrow you got free for hauling it away just needs a steel bar here, a brace there, new babbitt in the bearings, and it's ready for your rock patch.

About pouring bearings: I have been able to acquire good, solid machinery, from sorghum mills to cutoff saws and woodworking machines, cheap becase the bearings were worn out. Pouring bearings is like most of blacksmithing: There's no magic at all, just a little horse sense.

POURING BEARING BLOCK

HOT BABBIT POURED
INTO SPACE BETWEEN
SHAFT AND
BEARING BLOCK

SHAFT

BLOCK

OPEN ENDS STOPPED
WITH WET SAND

You need some babbitt, which most junkyards have, pryable out of rusting bearing blocks. And something to melt it in, which doesn't take much heat (I've done it over a fire of wood chips).

I pour the babbit with the bearing block and shaft, if possible, set in place in damp sand. I use a cast-iron ladle heated in the forge. The stuff cools quickly, then I remove the block and repeat with the bearing cap, shaft again in place, ends stopped with sand. If the block and shaft can't be removed from the machinery easily, you can use a caulking made of clay, or buy some commercial waxy stuff the old-timers called "bear grease" to seal the ends, and pour while in place. Most older equipment bearings allow for shims, to be removed as they wear. I cut these from tin cans. And pour with the shims in place, to allow for more babbitt than you need, against wear. New oil holes can be drilled easily, last.

We've talked about chainmaking earlier. And while it's not a profitable pastime, it's good to be able to link up stray pieces you might have found or traded for.

Round rod is cheap at the steelyard, or you might find some at your friendly junkyard. The early blacksmiths used worn-out horseshoes and wagon tires to make their chain rod, working up a supply when things were slow. You can reduce almost any scrap to, say, a ⅜-inch rod, which is a good size for strong chain. I use about a 6½-inch length for each link, scarfed and looped and linked, with no particular attention paid to final shape until after it's welded. There's plenty of heat left to shape the link after the weld is made and the joint shaped. Remember to make the weld at the end of the link; it's stronger there than at the sides where machine-made chain is welded. Another thing I do is weld up, say, 3 feet of chain at a time, then join these pieces. It's easier than handling the entire length of chain every time you add one link.

Of course, here I am reminded of the old blacksmith's riddle of the man who brought five pieces of chain, of three links each, to the shop to have them joined, insisting that it could be done with only three cuts and three welds. The smith wanted to make, and charge him for, four. I'll leave that one for you to play with, and the answer makes my point about joining pieces.

Always keep short pieces of chain around to use with your ratchet cable hoist or winch. A good way to break a cable is to crimp it by hooking it around something and back to itself.

Another story I like is of the old farmers who bought the first arc-welded chain when it began to replace forged chain. Suspicious of the new welding method, many of them would wrap the new chain around a stump they were burning or toss it into a burning brushpile to heat and anneal. They wanted to make darn sure any hard spots were softened before the chain was put to use. "Better to stretch than break" is sound advice still.

Forge your chain hooks from heavier stock than the chain itself. I once came by a bucket of old railroad spikes that made excellent hooks. Use at least ⅝-inch bar for a ⅜-inch chain; otherwise the pull will straighten out the hook before the chain itself gives way. Hammer the point and loop that links to the chain out while straight, leaving heavy metal at what will become the curve of the hook. Bend the loop and weld it before you shape the hook, in case you blow it. That's a good rule if your forge welding is a bit uncertain; weld early before you've put too much time into the piece.

Now shape the hook over the anvil horn, hammering flat the flaring inner curve as you go. For a grab hook, lay the curved hook on its back on the anvil and drive the hook almost closed, then open from the tip on the horn. A grab hook should just slip over the chain thickness, with almost no clearance. Clamp a flat ⅜-inch thick bar in the vise and do the final fitting around it. A slip hook should be deep, since it's easy for the chain to flop out, so use more metal.

I like the crossbar at the end of a harness trace chain or any pull-chain hook. To forge it, upset the tip first, so you'll have plenty of metal to work with, then work the bar as you taper to the point. Again, do ev-

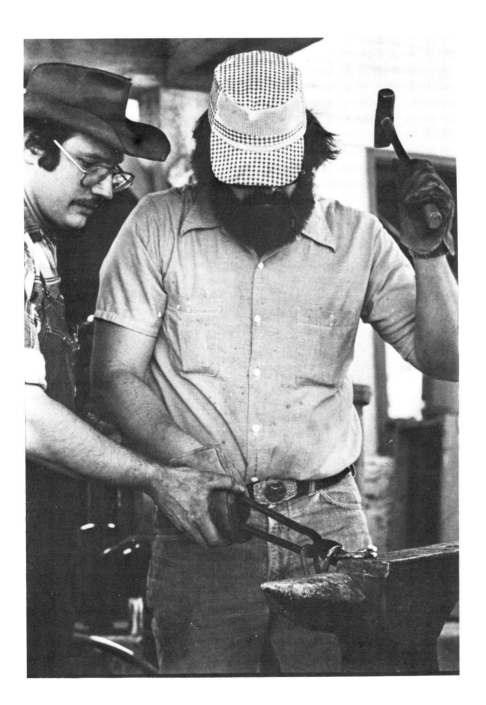

For a better chance of getting a good forge weld, go through it cold a few times. Here Wayne Haymes shows Bill Jennings how to hold the scarfed and lapped ends of a chin link for welding.

A punched-hole chain grab hook. First the bar is drawn out, fullered, and punched.

The half-bent hook is returned to the forge for a second heat. It would function this way as a slip hook, to let the chain slide in it.

The finished hook, with chain attached. Hooks must be heavier than their chain to keep from opening out in a pull. The grab hook holds across a chain link, not allowing it to slide.

Very nice T-bar chain hook and swivel from New England. These welds were made on the anvil horn after splitting the iron, leaving heavier metal at the wear points. T-bar was upset.

erything on a hook before you bend it, or you'll have an awkward shape to deal with.

The "boomer" or chain binder is a handy device that's going up in price fearsomely. I watch for broken ones I can buy cheap, then repair them. If you forge this tool and leave a hard place in it through poor tempering, the jolts it will take can dump a load of logs or a loaded tractor off on somebody when it snaps.

A boomer should break over center just right and hold properly, so if you forge one from stock, I'd say have a borrowed one handy to refer to as you go.

In my growing-up days we tightened chain around a load with a long pole through the slack, twisted around, and tied with baling wire. I've used the boomer to lift heavy objects, one chain link at a time, hooking my progress each time.

Do put a swivel next to each hook on the boomer. They're just about worthless without them. I picked up a good repaired one cheap once, because the smith who'd repaired it left out the swivels. He did do an interesting job on one hook, though, which had originally been the head of a pipewrench.

I always riveted chain swivels to make the head, until I saw the New England style on some old chain I brought back from there. These swivels were forged by splitting the heavily headed rod; then it was put through the punched hole, shaped to chain thickness, spread, and lap welded on the anvil horn. This results in swivels much stronger than those riveted. The riveted swivel also tends to spread and bind in the hole. The hole is punched in heavy stock, which is then drawn to chain thickness and lap welded over the head.

153

Knives find never-ending use around the farm. Hacking around your farmstead never seems finished—brush, briars, even tall weeds require a sturdy, keen blade to help keep your place from going totally back to the woods. The surplus-store machetes are usually made in Japan from old beer cans, or if they're good, are high-priced.

Spring steel, temper-drawn to a purple or blue, makes a good machete (corn knife). Another good one is tough car axle shaft, just quenched, if you'll take the time to hammer it flat. There are a variety of designs, including one with a sharpened hook on the backside for close cropping without stooping. I use two, a heavy, long (24-inch) one for lopping limbs, small trees and cutting briars at arm's length, and a Bowie knife, which is handy and much lighter. The Bowie serves as every other kind of knife, too. I use it a lot to rough shape tool handles before I drawknife them.

Knifemaking is another venture altogether if you want to pick up some cash selling them. Most knifemakers use expensive alloys and work cold, heat treating only after hours spent cutting, grinding, and belt-sanding. Then they mirror polish them to compete for the high prices collectors will pay.

I am often asked to forge knives, and I explain that I am a blacksmith, not a knifemaker. My concern is with forging steel, and I could care less about polishing out the forge and hammer marks. I want a blade of medium carbon that will cut, flex slightly without breaking, and hold a reasonable edge.

Folk tales abound about knives that split bolts, stones, other knives, and hard objects in general and still hold a razor edge. And, of course, these magic knives will bend double and return to their shape an infinite number of times.

The facts are these: A lasting cutting edge has to be hard. The harder it is, the more brittle it is and more prone to chip. The more given to flexing, the softer the metal. Of course, we now have sophisticated alloys for specific purposes, among them those of the stainless, no-rust character.

The magic folklore knife just doesn't exist. But really fine knives can be made from a variety of carbon steels or alloys; they just won't perform magic the way the aging town blowhard would have you believe. The best cutting edges, I still maintain, are to be had from carbon steel, soft enough not to chip, hard enough to last. The exact steel and tempering depend on the use the knife will get. A woodcarving knife is not a skinning knife is not a throwing knife.

I once watched a knifesmith impress the other rustics by shaving steel strips off a factory cold chisel with one of his knives. Of course, that particular knife, no doubt quenched hard, was not for sale, and probably would have shattered if dropped on the sidewalk. His other knives were

Wayne Haymes points out areas to be draw filed while this hammered knife blade is annealed, to farrier Jay Andrews and silversmith Ginny Ward during a course in blacksmithing Wayne helped me teach.

A vegetable chopping knife being shaped while annealed, and a finished Bowie knife, both of spring steel.

acceptably flexible and, I'm sure, quite serviceable, but not for shaving chisels. I really don't know if he'd annealed that chisel or not. He probably had.

You can buy factory-made hunting knives for much less than the time investment you'll have in forging them, or for the price you'd have to charge a customer. But here again is that perfectly valid mystique of the hand-forged tool that lets us blacksmiths survive. Nobody's grandchildren gaze in awed admiration at a knife that's still available downtown, cheap. Remember that each knife you make is unlike any other in existence; thank Heaven for hand craftsmanship.

I like to hammer a knife to a state that requires little filing or grinding. The flatter is useful here, to leave a nearly dent-free surface. I have to know what a knife is to be used for before I start, and select the steel and temper to that use. It may be evenly tempered, or hard at the edge and quite soft at the spine. I may sacrifice edge-holding for flexibility, as with a throwing knife or machete that gets jolted a lot.

I use a steel anywhere from 30-point to 80-point carbon. Never have I tried to use an old file, which just isn't very good steel for a knife (it's dandy for a file, and was often the only steel the old-timers could get that they knew was high carbon). Knifesmiths mostly lean toward 4140 or D2 carbon or the 440 stainless group of alloys. These are medium carbon, and have some nice characteristics. Remember, these last two numbers often denote carbon content.

I always quench a knife in oil to avoid cracking. Warping, too, is lessened with oil. If a knife warps, you can go ahead and draw the temper, then cold hammer the convex surface with it flat on the anvil to straighten it. Stresses in the steel are relieved this way, too, and if you've done your job right, you will not break the blade. If you've blown it, you will again, and will shatter the knife. So start over. Quenching straight down in the oil will usually forestall warping.

Knifemaking is a high craft form, so experiment around with steels and tempering before you call yourself a knifesmith. I'm perfectly content to avoid that label, though a lot of my knives are skinning creatures, carving wood and hacking brush around the hills at this moment.

Another thing I'm not, I find, is a farmer. I just have no talent in that direction, although I spend a lot of time helping build or repairing implements for folks around me who are. If you dig in the soil, you'll keep your forge forever busy.

And as I said earlier, the extent of your work with your place in the country will bear a direct relation to the time you spend working iron.

So hammer your way toward the goal of independence, whether you ever actually arrive or not.

CHAPTER TEN

The Farrier's Craft

I cannot tell you how many times I have been accused of not being a "real" blacksmith because I don't shoe horses. In the memories of the living generations, most country blacksmiths, driven by the machine age to accepting any kind and all kinds of work to survive, shod horses. And that picture has become fixed in the minds of just about everybody, except smiths and some farriers.

"Sure is a funny-looking horseshoe you're making," calls the crafts center wag, popcorn in hand and mind left safely at home, to the blacksmith sweating over a trivet or scroll.

"You think this horseshoe looks funny, you should see the horse it goes on. He's a real mess." Rehearsed good humor, although the smith would rather say something else entirely.

In pure fact, shoeing horses requires a knowledge of the animals and their physiology completely foreign to iron. And conversely, few working farriers know the mysteries of tempering steels and the wide range of other smithing practices.

But the myth persists. Those old-timers *saw* every country smith shoe horses, and you just ain't a blacksmith unless you do it too, sonny. No good explaining that horse owners and professional farriers did most of the shoeing up until the general smith got into it too, maybe 150 years ago. Anyway, what does it matter?

"Well, the real reason I don't shoe horses," I'd confide to the crafts center crowd, "is this deep-seated mistrust of horses." I'd prop my foot on the anvil block. "You see, one threw me once, years ago. . . ."

Ah! Psychological stuff, right off the TV soaps; they're on home ground, they begin to nod sagely. ". . . and I landed on my face right in these sharp flintrocks. Well, it took out a whole big piece of my cheek, see, and I went to the doctor."

"You're gonna have to have a skin graft, Mac," he said.

"Fine, whose do we use? Maybe somebody without too much acne . . ."

"No, no, we have to use yours. Pick a spot where you'll miss it the least."

"Well, I thought about that some, and decided my rear end was the safest spot. So that's where he took it, and he patched up my face. And you can't hardly tell it now, can you?"

"Sure did a nice job. So that's why he don't like horses. Does he really mean all that? These flintrocks'll sure cut you. . . ." nods, mutters.

"So now when my mother-in-law visits and kisses me on that cheek, I just smile. . . ." Back to the anvil.

In fact, being a neighborhood farrier is a good way to make a few dollars. There are an awful lot of horses in the country today; someone recently told me there are more now than in horse-and-buggy days. Maybe so. The folks who own horses usually own several, and there are lots more folks today. Someone has to shoe those horses, particularly if they're to be ridden, worked, or shown. Lots of people have theirs shod in any case to protect the hooves from excessive splitting and pasture-stone damage.

So we'll talk about the farrier's craft, which could become a very real part of your homesteading if you elect to go into horse-powered pursuits. And for your own animals, my brother John, who's his rural neighborhood farrier as well as a farmer and a smith, has some good advice:

Some of the farrier's tools made by Jay Andrews of Springfield, Missouri, during a blacksmith course I taught.

Before you buy any horse for any use, have his feet looked at carefully by a good farrier. No need to set yourself up for a continuing problem of corrective shoeing, unless you happen to be good at it. Too many prespective buyers ignore the feet, which may not show in gait if shod correctly.

Another bit of advice: Get to know a farrier, and weasel some way to be his apprentice for a time if you're serious about this. You'll either give it up or learn it well. You can enroll in a farrier's school, too, of which there are several good ones across the country, but they aren't cheap. The schools will usually teach you hot shoeing, and basic blacksmithing, but you already know that. Some farriers never heat a shoe to work it, but do it all cold. Bending the point of a barred shoe cold is no good, though, so apply your forging knowledge to the teachings of a cold-shoe farrier.

A good shoer makes it look easy. Bob Peters of Berryville, Arkansas, can shoe thirty horses a day, partly because he's an experienced professional, partly because he's built close to the ground, and a powerful, stocky man.

"Couldn't shoe ten if I had to bend my back," he says. His hands move with no apparent effort, and the hoof is pared, trimmed, rasped, an apprentice often handing him tools and helping hold a restive horse. The shoe goes on with a few lightning hammer blows, with those wicked nail points twisted off sort of in the same motion as the last stroke. The clinches are made and rasped smooth while Bob talks horses to his client and reassurances to the animal. A quick rasp around above the new shoe leaves it all smooth and fitted, and the hoof is let down.

Jay Andrews of Springfield, Missouri, is a young farrier, a graduate of a Midwest school. His equipment is complete, down to a gas forge in his pickup bed. His approach is also professional, though somewhat more measured and methodical. Like all farriers, these men have a rapport with the animals that is instantly evident. Without that, you would never be a farrier.

But I wanted to watch a homesteader at work, not a professional, so I went over to my brother John's place to see a typical farm shoeing. He was to put shoes on his Arabian mare, who has some registered name, but his teen-age kids call her Dad's Root Beer, partly for her color, a foam white flecked with brown.

Well, Root Beer had borne a foal and run free over a year unshod, down in the creek-bottom fields. So her hooves were chipped and split pretty deeply, but John said that's natural, and a couple of shoeings would even everything out again. His sixteen-year-old daughter Maria wanted to work with the mare—a very fast horse—hence the shoeing.

John has an empathy with animals that once enabled him to calm a wounded deer, then carry it single-handedly out of the woods for doctoring. His horses are like faithful dogs with him, which makes shoeing easier.

First Root Beer was tied loosely to a tree, then John wiped some insect repellent on her legs to lessen a tendency to kick at flies. Then he picked rocks and bits of wood from her front hoof with a hoof pick that he had forged from a worn-out horseshoe. Next he explored the entire bottom surface of the foot with the hoof knife, paring here and there to remove dead horn and look for problem areas. Satisfied, he used the nippers to clip off excess growth of the outer shell of horn, which is more like trimming fingernails than anything else. He didn't try to cut to the depth of the broken-out places, which might get down to sensitive tissue. The bottom surface of the hoof was rasped flat, then, and a shoe of the right size tried. This mare took a No. 1 shoe, but it was obvious that it would need work.

John uses a homemade shoeing anvil on a heavy spike for shoeing, and except for corrective work or specialty shoes, he shapes them cold. They're low enough in carbon that they can be hardened only a little by quenching from red, so aren't that difficult to shape cold. A barred or caulked shoe he would have worked hot.

The shoe is fitted so that the line of recessed nail holes falls just outside the white line of cartilaginous growth inside the outer horn. The nails are prebent to follow a path to the outside of the hoof, so of course there's a right way and a wrong way to drive them. Sometimes, too, the prepunched nail holes in the shoe will have some iron left in them, which can be cleaned up with the pritchel (square-hole punch).

The shoe is held in place with one nail started, then another is driven across the hoof from it. Hammer blows must be light and quick, since this is the part the horse enjoys least. The instant each nail is driven, the shoer is holding a deadly weapon in his hand. The pointed nail, sharper than a lot of knives, is curving out of the side of the hoof maybe an inch. I have seen fingers laid open, legs ripped, and even the tough leather apron of the shoer torn when the horse decides it wants its foot back on the ground at this point, thank you.

John has developed an extra quick hammer stroke, switched to the nail point that bends the nail down almost parallel to the hoof. Horses obviously know when you're through hammering, and they often wait till then to jerk the foot away.

Now, even bent down, that projecting sharpie has to come off quickly. Some shoers use the clinch cutters to nip it, some slip the hammer claws around it and twist it off. The object is to get the hoof disarmed, fast. Subsequent nails are cut as driven. If the farrier hasn't let the horse put its foot down for a while, it's a good idea now. It gives the farrier a chance to straighten up, too.

Next, a small burr of cut horn fibers will have been pushed out by

Some working farrier tools. From left on top they are clinch knife, clinch cutters (or nail cutters), hoof pick, hoof knife, hoof nippers, rasp, pritchel, shoeing hammer, and alligator. At the bottom are 3-pound forging hammer, leather apron, factory and hand-forged shoes, and ball-peen hammer.

the emerging nail, and this should be cut off with the corner of a file somewhat finer than the rasp. A little horizontal groove is made just under the cut-off nail, so when the nail is clinched it won't tend to start a split in the hoof.

Some farriers use the clinch cutters held closed, butted up against the nailhead, while they clinch the end with the hammer. Others use an alligator, which looks like tongs with one jaw bent out in a curve with sawtooth grooves across it. John made his from worn clinch cutters, but they can be had new. The flat jaw holds the nailhead, while the bent-jaw serrations catch and clinch the cut end. A little more pressure and the hardened serrations slip, shaving the clinched end smoother. These ends

161

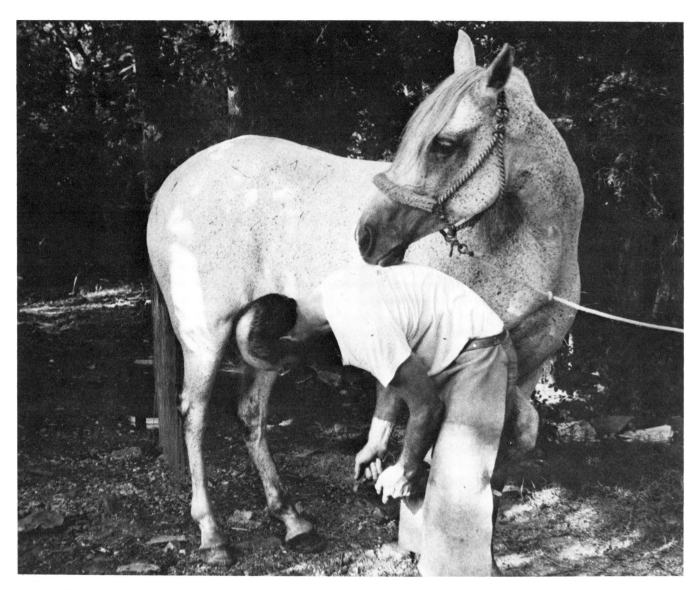

John McRaven prepares to shoe his mare. John is a neighborhood farrier around his farm at Hilda, Missouri.

should then be rasped, or the horse can hurt itself, hang up in fences, or hurt other animals, including you.

John gives his mare's hoof a final rasping to take off any overhanging horn, and the foot is shod. He likes to start with a front foot, then work around both back ones, to finish "with another easy one" at the front.

Had there been old shoes on, he would have used the clinch knife, driven flat between shoe and hoof to shear the old nails off, then cut off the old clinches and pulled the nails with the cutters. Or he could cut off the clinches and get the cutters under the branches of the shoe to pull it as he clamped.

Horses in flintrock country go through shoes fairly fast, so most folks put caulked shoes with toe bars on. John usually uses a hard-surfacing electrode to arc weld three humps at the toe for wear, since that's where it's heaviest.

Stones are removed with the hoof pick.

The curved hoof knife pares away dead horn.

"Makes it easy to track my horses if they get out, too," he says.

The list of specialty shoes that have or have had practical applications goes on and on. One old-timer once offered to show me seventy-eight kinds. I got lost after a dozen or so. There are toe bars to be welded on, drive caulks, caulks made simply by bending the shoe's metal ends for more iron.

But as I said earlier, unless you've bought yourself some problems in the horse or in the location of your homestead, standard shoeing practices should do. You can, of course, make your own shoes from stock, using bar mild steel or low-carbon, 5/16 to ⅜ inch thick, ¾ inch wide, and about a foot long for a start.

I cut the nailhead grooves while the bar is straight, using the hot chisel. I understand farrier's suppliers have curved chisels for this. Use a store horseshoe for a pattern, and heat and bend to shape. Start at the center, or toe, and work to the sides, or branches. You'll find that front shoes need different shaping from back ones, so you might as well get them as nearly right as you can while you hammer them.

Use the pritchel to punch the nail holes, four to a side, and try to space them differently. One problem with machine-made shoes is that the nail always goes in right over the old nail hole, and the hoof horn is weaker there. Angle the pritchel so that the nail hole will lead the nail outward through the hoof wall.

Hoof nippers are used to trim excess horn and even it out to take the shoe.

The bottom of the hoof is rasped for a flat surface.

Now round the ends of the shoes after you've determined the length, by close hammering, or you can heat, clamp in the vice, and rasp them hot. Don't toss the shoe into the tub if it has any carbon content to speak of. You'll be bending it a bit here and there later, so keep it soft until it's the right shape. Let it cool somewhere away from the reach of small children. Everyone knows the story of the smith who was plagued by the village smart-aleck, a stripling who always got the last word. The smith had just completed a set of shoes for the farrier, and had left them on the anvil to cool. They looked innocent enough, at black heat, as the irritating fellow made his routine entrance.

John uses standard shoes, but builds up three spots of hard-surface electric welding rod at the toe, on his own horses.

The shoe is nailed with the nails slanted outward at just the right angle to emerge from the outside horn at the right height.

The sharp shank of the nail is either twisted off as here, or cut with nail cutters, as soon as it is driven.

165

This tool, called an alligator, clinches the nail, and shears off some of the ragged cut end. A horizontal groove has been cut just below with the file.

The nail ends are finished off with the rasp, and the hoof is smoothed even with the shoe all around, to finish the job.

"Now don't you start," the smith held up his hand, "until I've got your advice on something. You bein' a man that gets around among th' gentlefolk a lot, I want you to check over those shoes I made for the judge's mare, and tell me if you think they're good enough."

Well. Entrusted with the function of Quality Control Supervisor (he could see the name in Barnum script), the lad approached the anvil and, of course, picked up a shoe. Then with a howl he dropped it and plunged hand and arm into the slack tub, amid the roars from the smith and assorted gathered town worthies.

"What's the matter, son, was that shoe still hot?" queried the smith, in a vain effort at solicitation.

"No," gritted the youth, then righting himself and adjusting his straw boater before marching out, "it just don't take a man like me long to look at a horseshoe."

For my own part, I doubt if I'll even undertake shoeing horses, unless forced by grim economic necessity to run my life around them. If that happens, I'll have to get on a lot more familiar and trusting basis with them first. That big an animal can cause a lot of damage just accidentally.

Besides shoeing, there are many other smithing aspects to the world of the horse. There's harness, with buckles, rings, chains, and hooks. There is the need for ironwork in building, repairing, or maintaining everything the horse moves, from plow to sleigh. Man and horse had a long working relationship on the small homestead for many hundreds of years, and there are some quite good points for the arrangement.

One thing you will be able to count on is a lot of work hammering the iron you and the horse will wear out over the years. And shucks, then you'll be a "real" blacksmith, too.

CHAPTER ELEVEN

Income from Your Forge

First of all, if you have any ideas of slipping into the role of the old-time blacksmith and earning a living by the sweat of your hammer like Great-Grandpa did, you can just about forget the whole thing.

The economics of competing with machine-made ironwork drove the old blacksmith out of business. First, he broadened the range of the jobs he did. I mentioned horseshoeing earlier, and wheelwrighting was another common area. Lots of village smiths were also the local dentists, pulling teeth by hand or tongs. Certainly this man who made the early dentist's tools knew something of their use. The smith made coffins, too, and occasionally tinware, and he expanded his smithy sometimes to make room for a foundry operation.

But it was a losing game. One by one the old shops closed, the ranks of thousands of smiths thinned by age, or by their going into new specialized fields: The welder, the machinist, the mechanic were former smiths. So were many of the farriers, obliged by the changing times to become traveling craftsmen.

A few smiths, such as the great Samuel Yellin of Philadelphia, attained an excellence in decorative work that exceeded anything the machine-makers could produce, and continued a thriving business. I have read that Yellin had as many as three hundred smiths working for him at the height of his productivity in the second quarter of this century.

Others specialized in gunsmithing, or in fine cutlery, or in one-of-a-kind tools of carbon steel for discriminating buyers. Indeed, these two forge products—decorative ironwork and hand-forged tools—seem to be about the only ones saleable at a profit today.

You just can't make it by sharpening plow points and making chain. The rare individual who wants forged chain will elevate his eyebrows at the $1.00-plus per link you'd have to charge. And even the sign bracket you labored over, drawn and scrolled, riveted and graceful, can be had cheaper done cold and arc welded by the ornamental iron shop that turns them out by the thousands.

True, there are those few people who want and will pay for art in iron. But you must know you will be joining the ranks of artists and craftspeople starving all across the land today, competing for sales to these few. Potters, painters, sculptors, leatherworkers, furniture-makers— talk to them about their customers, and about the lookers, whose houses are full of plastic and who can't tell the difference. And while you may be the only blacksmith at, say, a major crafts event, you'll face the same general indifference to handmade work as these other creative people do. The public is so conditioned to machine-made duplication, most buyers really can't understand that your work is all done by you, and that each piece is unique.

I'm reminded of my friend sculptor Dennis Thompson, who's fascinated with dragons. Powerful, intricately sculptured dragons with each of hundreds of body scales attached separately, each porcelain tooth shaped and inserted—art in a very high form. At an art show once, a slow day, nobody buying, a woman tapped one.

"Is that clay?" she asked.

"Yes, ma'am, it is."

"Well, it's made in a mold, of course, then."

"No, ma'am, I built it all by hand." Patiently (how many thousand times had he said this to people?). First of all, no mold could enclose those shapes, and second, how would you get just the porcelain down into the claws and teeth, and then . . . oh, never mind. The woman was indignant.

"You can't expect *me* to believe that wasn't done in a mold, young man," and she turned to leave.

"Well, all right, lady, I'll admit it was done in a mold, but that mold"—he shook a finger in her face—"that mold was a real son-of-a-bitch to build!"

We have one of Dennis's dragons, but he refuses to let me see the fabled mold.

My commercial work consists mainly of tools, mostly of an antique nature. Drawknives, froes, and broadaxes sell, as do some more present-day useful tools. I can always sell a digging bar or prybar of carbon steel with a chisel point. Or a tempered punch or cold chisel, if cheap enough. Buyers want to be able to brag about handwork, and as in the old days, will attribute almost magical qualities to the steel you've hammered, especially if they've watched you do it.

At a crafts fair I can almost always sell a fireplace poker or potrack I've made right there before the onlookers' eyes. Or, as often, I can take a custom order for one just a little different to suit a particular taste or need. In the matter of punches and chisels, showing the magic of hardening and tempering never fails to draw a throng of handymen. Then a scornful

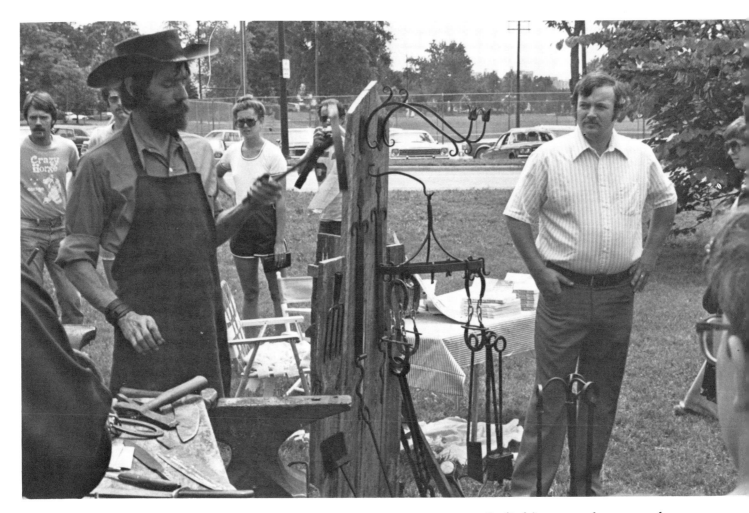

Crafts fairs are good money-makers. I've just demonstrated a hoop weld here, amid a display of knives, fireplace tools, potracks, hinges, sconces and lots of other pieces.

comparison of your work, of selected carbon steel with hardness graded to its use, against those machine-shaped, mass-quenched offerings of the hardware store, will generate some sales. I hint at the doubtful origins of factory-produced tools, and have been known to accuse those villains of recycling beer cans to make cold chisels.

The fair circuit is fun, but it's hard work. You need a portable set-up, with a small anvil and light forge. You'll get into some good fairs because your demonstrations will bring crowds, and the local media will zero in on your colorful setup. But be prepared for endless and dumb questions, and prepare to learn that everybody's grandfather was a smith. Only a *real* smith (better than you).

So many fairgoers are there to be entertained, not to buy. Many will buy trinkets or souvenirs, and you can make your entry fee back by selling things like hand-forged nails at $.50 or pothooks for $1.50 or $2.00.

You will sell or trade pieces to the other exhibitors, who are largely appreciative of this kind of work, and often delightful people. The camaraderie at a favorite annual fair is as big a reason for my participating as the prospect of sales.

Selling through other shops puts you into the wholesale production business, and handwork is hard to wholesale profitably. A good smith I know went this route, and was broke in a year. The standard price around the Midwest is 50 percent of the retail, and shopowners will try to get you to lower your price more so the pieces will move.

Consignment is an inhuman way for the craftsman to sell. Percentages to the retailers are high—30 to 50 percent—and there's no money till the eventual sale. In the meantime, things get lost or shoplifted, and you have no money to buy iron with—let alone food.

You *can* go into mass production and cut prices and quality to compete for the vacationer's dollar. But of course you're then no longer a blacksmith. You can also make each piece the only one of its kind—art in iron—and price it accordingly for that rare buyer who must be out there somewhere. And be assured that you have not compromised your art, as the utility bills and the rent come due and your stomach growls.

That's why so many blacksmiths are hobbyists today. Making a living at it means moving fast, and leaving no stone unturned. The smiths I know who're not salaried by crafts centers, do some of everything to make it, as the old-timers had to.

I teach workshops, do crafts fairs, appear at school programs and civic clubs, write articles about blacksmithing, and make just about anything a customer wants, from current orders for a set of kitchen knives to a massive rake for grubbing flintrock. And I can't begin to make a living from my forge. If I placed pieces in all the crafts shops in the region, the law of averages would lose some for me, make some enemies for me, work me mercilessly, sell some for me, and I might make a sort of living at it.

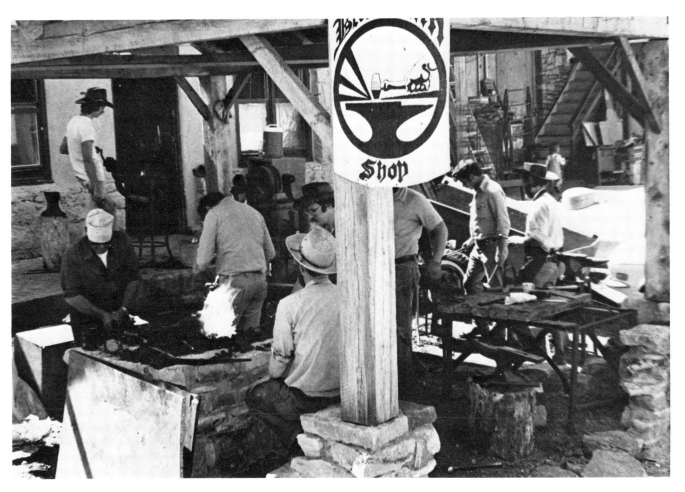

I often teach courses in blacksmithing. Here Wayne Haymes and I give instruction to students at the Hollister, Missouri, shop.

Here Ginny Ward, a silversmith, puts a finishing curl on the tulip candle holder of a chandelier arm. This was a blacksmithing school project.

I do an odd job for a farmer now and then, like forge a digging bar or a hook he can't find in the hardware store. And welding-shop owners will bring me a problem they aren't sure about, usually having to do with carbon steel. (Why does the spring steel keep breaking right next to my weld? Because the cold steel next to it is chilling it and making it brittle.)

A good connection is with one or more antique shops. Missing hardware is common, and I do pieces for old furniture, primitives, and collectibles I don't know the names of. Custom-furniture-makers are also good people to work with—the very nature of their work and their clientele fit with your forgework.

Craft centers often hire smiths during tourist season. This is

Repairing antiques can be a good business. This primitive set of wagon-tire andirons had separated at forge welds in two places.

Triangle dinner gongs sell well and are quickly made of ½-inch mild steel, but have a sharper ring if of higher carbon stock, such as this one of shafting.

173

show-off work, mostly, and you get tired of answering incredible questions. But I did learn more than forge welding from Shad Heller, who's been the star attraction of the craft center near my Missouri home for twenty years, and knows his smithing.

Bob Patrick has earned his living as a smith for a dozen years now. He teaches almost constantly, working on his own and through the local arts council. Craft centers hire him for workshops, too. And his ornamental work is among the best I've seen.

Wayne Haymes ran his shop in Hollister, Missouri, full-time, supplying fireplace sets, triangle gongs, and horseshoe puzzles to retailers in quantity. He also did custom work, from boot scrapers to belt buckles. But he eventually had to take a regular job, smithing now only on days off and as special orders require.

Many smiths double in welding or as mechanics or farriers, just as they would have in 1900. There is seldom enough work to pay rent and overhead for a commercial operation, unless you're a hustler and a good salesman, too.

But your farmstead shop should be free of such overhead beyond your time, a few sacks of coal, and the odd purchases of iron. Let it become known around the rural community that you're hammering out things that can't be bought over any counter, or providing services of a

Curving the heated chisel by hammering it against the step of the anvil.

Blacksmithing is finished on a woodcarver's chisel. The metal collar and ridges will hold a wooden handle in place.

A commercial job for another smith. Heating this anvil in order to harden it required most of an afternoon, then it nearly boiled the slack tub dry in quenching. The chain is to lift it by.

Another commercial job for another smith. This is the upset ball at the end of a vise bar handle. The second ball has to be forged with the vise screw in place.

special nature, and you'll have a few jobs soon. A replacement drawbar for an old tractor, a set of harness hooks for a prize team of Clydesdales, a potrack to fit in an awkward part of the kitchen, an axe retempered, bush hog blades to be resharpened and to be heat treated.

You may not make much money, but you'll be able to support your shop easily, and perform a service for the area. And make some friends, because you'll find country people have a liking and respect for anyone who can do things with his hands and isn't afraid to work.

The overriding question regarding selling your work is what to charge for it. Every craftsperson has to work that one out for himself, and not being able to is a big reason a lot of them don't make it.

First of all, you must establish a cost of doing business. Even if your overhead is pennies, you must figure the value of your time, replacement of worn equipment, and cost of additional equipment. All this goes with coal cost, iron cost, transportation, and electricity to determine a shop cost per hour.

Automobile repair shops and welding shops may charge $15 to $20 per hour shop time, to be added to parts cost. Why should your smithy, specializing as it does, charge less? At $15 an hour, a project that takes half a day would be $60. Add material cost of, say, $10, since your products are the result mostly of labor.

Four hours is about right for a 36-inch pair of well-made strap hinges, or a fireplace set of poker, shovel, tongs, and stand. Or a potrack with maybe twenty hooks. If the buyer wants the pieces hand forged, he'll pay the $70 for them. If, down deep, he really doesn't care that much, if he's bargain-hunting and would just as soon buy from the discount store, he's at the wrong place.

If it's important to a buyer that a piece be one-of-a-kind work, it's worth a good price. It's an heirloom. Don't try to compete with the machine age. You don't make any friends, nor any profit, by cutting prices. I think I'm typical when I buy handwork: If I see good craftsmanship, price is no longer the question.

Another way to determine price is to set a figure you must be paid for your time. If you can work for $50 a day clear, you might charge only $25 plus for that four-hour job. Since you won't work every day all day, you'll have to hedge that figure, though—say, double—for the time you can't be at the shop hammering.

My own time is worth a certain figure to me, arrived at by considering the rate I'd be drawing for consulting work, restoration work, courses, workshops, and writing. I will take a block of that time to make a piece for someone who appreciates it, but only for a comparable rate, plus overhead. It has worked well for me, because I now have enough projects going so that if I don't do the forgework, I'll spend that block of time on one of the other pursuits, for income.

Splitting the end of a wrought-iron fireplace arch brace to make a pot rack. Possibly originally a case-hardened buggy axle, this iron was almost too tough to hacksaw.

The completed pot rack, which will be mounted on a heavy horizontal beam with large lag bolts. Hooks are of ½-inch square stock, single and split double.

I've just finished a pair of $250 andirons on that basis. No other smith I know would charge that much for a relatively simple (graceful, yes) design, but the owners are ecstatic. They looked at it as buying art, this art being useful, too.

Whatever you charge, be it dollars, in-kind work, or trades for vegetables and eggs, approach your work at the forge as your specialty, your contribution to the well-being of the rural community. Don't sell it short, and neither will anybody else.

Realize, too, that you are one of a quite select scattering of craftspeople, practitioners of the mighty craft that produced the tools for just about all the rest of them. And be just a little proud.

CHAPTER TWELVE

Prospects

Your prospects as a blacksmith today are good, all things considered, whether you plan to set up a commercial operation or not. Even as a hobby, the craft will allow you to create useful and artistic pieces for your own home and shop, and those of friends. There's a wider appreciation now for things handmade than when we were all in love with the Industrial Revolution.

The people I train who are going on to make their livings from smithing are usually either specializing in ornamental iron or tools, for instance, or combining forge work with general welding and other metal work, to offer a range of services.

Rural areas are excellent for this kind of setup. Neighboring farmers with obsolete equipment can't get replacement parts at the dealership. Often the machine shop or welding shop in town can't or won't make repairs, or their prices are too high. You won't have their overhead, and you'll also be able to create and shape parts these other shops can't. And rural neighbors will patronize you because you're there, once they get to know you.

And when custom orders lag, which they will, you can put your skills to work on such projects as building farm wagons and utility trailers, repairing worn or broken tools and equipment for resale. The ability to use the forge, for one thing, and a knowledge of carbon steels (forging and welding), for another, will make it possible for you to produce quality work cheaply.

A few stock items such as splitting mauls, digging bars, tow chains, cant hooks, re-drawn and tempered pickaxes, cold chisels, can be kept on hand for sale at a good profit. Fabricated trailers, sleds, truck beds can be made sturdy with forged bracing, usually with recycled, free iron.

Your advantage over the commercial welding or machine shop in town will be that you're close by, first. And also it's often the case that a part or piece that can't very well be milled or turned or arc-welded, can be hammered, and maybe hardened and tempered. And your hammering will almost always be far cheaper than the machinist's complicated setup time, or the welder's multiple cuts and welds to produce the same piece (if they can do it at all).

Every smith has his specialty. I happen to do more carbon steel work (tools, knives) than anything else. Two of the most successful working blacksmiths I know both do decorative iron, almost exclusively. Another has gone mostly into custom knife work, others are gunsmiths or farriers, having gone on from general working in iron.

Whatever becomes your own specialization, if you do it commercially, you must make clear to your customers that each piece of forge work is the only one there is like that. And that it's going to be around for generations, a sort of heirloom, like other forms of art. And that its price has got to befit such an effort. Your work doesn't compete with the cold-curled, spot-welded, spray-painted twisties of the local carport-post and porch-railing shop, so neither will your prices.

It could get to be a lonely business.

But aside from commercial pursuits, the forge will let you do the thousands of projects on your own place better, cheaper, faster. One of my recent Virginia students wanted to replace 20 forged shutter latches lost or rusted away on the ante-bellum house he was restoring. Only a blacksmith could produce those latches, duplicating the remaining originals.

Another former student is always finding things like only one of a set of really unique forged hinges at sales, antique shops. He's now duplicating these, turning his idle collection into usable hardware for his farm buildings. He's even discovered that a little judicious burning of the iron in the forge makes it look really old—instant rust.

Another man I knew in Missouri operated a sawmill for many years that he and his blacksmith brother built entirely from junkyard parts. Dog hook handles were old piston rods, the carriage setworks ratchet wheel was a castoff automobile flywheel. Framing was part wood, braced with old straps, shafts, bars. It was a case of rural necessity, coupled with imagination, and that skill with the hammer and the hot iron.

The original and unique pieces you can forge are endless. I've just finished a six-foot potrack for a friend's new house, made from an old, forged 1780's fireplace arch brace. I matched in design the forged hinges he and I had done for his doors. Such a piece, fitted with single and double pot hooks, could only have been done in the forge, by a hand process that did honor to the fine old piece of wrought iron we started with.

The value of the forge is made evident again every time I teach a workshop. Each student invariably brings to class several old tools or special projects from home to work on. Nothing demonstrates the practicality of the craft better than using these as class projects.

Take a worn pick head, for example. Often a student will bring one that is either too blunt to use or that has been drawn out so much there's no metal left. If there's steel to draw, we heat and hammer it out, taking care to work it only within the heat range from cherry red to yellow to protect the carbon steel. Then it's sharpened, hardened and tempered for use, usually to a bronze for this high carbon steel.

If the stub of the pick is too little to draw out, we cut and shape a length of heavy coil spring. Then if we're far enough along to get into forge welding, we try a lap weld, though this isn't an easy one to make. Or we might short-cut by heating both the new point and the pick head, then arc-welding them. The pre-heating keeps the mass of otherwise cold steel from cooling the weld and metal near it too quickly (almost like a quench), and keeps it from cracking. Then we harden and temper normally.

The value of this exercise is that it utilizes several smithing procedures in one useful project.

I never have students do "make-work" projects. Everything has its use. Even a forged chain link will perhaps join a hammered hook to a piece of chain found along the roadside or bought in a box of odds and ends at a flea market.

At any given time I can list a dozen or so forged pieces I've done within, say, the past week for my place. At this writing they'd be:

A slender, sharp punch for pre-punching nail holes in the sheet metal roof for my garage. A new bar handle for the vise I traded for. Braces for the wooden sides of my utility trailer. Pot hooks for cast-iron cookware in our kitchen. A new machete for hacking the briars and honeysuckle jungle. A miniature cleaver for my wife to chop vegetables with. New round-hole punches for use in the smithy itself. A pair of footrests for the antique wood-burner we heat with. A new fire shovel so I won't have to borrow the coal shovel from the shop any more. A basket-twist handle for a friend's antique cast-iron teakettle in trade for the use of his air compressor and sandblaster to get ahead of the rust on an antique car of mine, for which I'll soon forge new bumper braces and other irreplaceable parts.

For many modern smiths, the craft is simply a fascinating step beyond the woodworking shop or the garage fix-it bench. The difference, and most of the mystique, is that there are almost no limits to the smithy. You can actually forge the tools for any other craft I can think of, even the wrenches for fixing a sick engine, if you want to go that far. Or even (are you ready for this?) hammer out an entire engine itself. (How do you think the first ones were made?)

Just how far you go with your hammer in hand is up to no one but you. As your skill increases, you'll want to tackle more complex problems: Can you really build a pulled road scraper for that half-mile of potholes to your place? Sure. An old pickup axle or two, a cutout pipeline section for the blade, edged with castoff grader cutting edge, gears, racks, pinions from the junkyard . . .

Or your own woodstove, of maybe a small, test-rejected pressure tank, with forged fire door hinges, scrolled feet . . . Or your own plow or spike harrow or rock rake or earth-moving scoop. Or your own water-wheel for power generator or irrigation pump, down on the creek.

You see, until this age of punched-out, stamped, assembly-lined, robot-assembled, obsolescence-riddled throwaways, everything iron was made in the forge.

It still can be.

A final note: Don't let the assorted name-dropping sages get away with calling you "Smithy" (it's like being called a garage). Everybody seems able to remember and misinterpret Longfellow's first lines about the chestnut tree, but not the next line. Sometimes I roar at them (one was a Ph.D. in English, yet): "THE SMITH, A MIGHTY MAN IS HE . . ."

But at 140 pounds wringing wet, somehow I hardly fit the picture.

Glossary

Acetylene	Gas used with oxygen to weld or cut iron/steel.
Andirons	Metal supports for logs in a fireplace.
Anneal	To soften metal. Steel is softened by heating then cooling very slowly.
Anvil	Shaped surface of heavy steel on which hot metal is hammered.
Arc weld	Electric welding method to fuse two metals.
Ash dump	Device for cleaning ashes from forge.
Auger	Boring bit for making holes in wood.
Babbitt	Soft metal used in bearings.
Ball peen hammer	Hammer with a rounded back face.
Barking spud	Tool for peeling bark from logs.
Bearing	Device allowing free turning of a shaft or wheel.
Bellows	Flexible, valved enclosure for forcing air into the forge.
Blacksmithing	Working iron or steel.
Boomer	Chain binder or tightener.
Borax	Substance used as welding flux to seal out oxygen, which forms scale.
Brazing	Joining with molten bronze or brass.
Brine	Salt water, often used to quench and harden hot steel.
Butt weld	Joint made by forging two white-hot ends together.
Cant hook	Handled hook for moving logs.
Carbon content	Amount or degree of carbon in steel.
Carbon steel (tool steel)	Steel that has enough carbon content to harden for use as tools.
Case hardening	Making steel out of iron by letting it absorb carbon on the surface.
Chain binder	Device for hooking and tightening chain.
Charcoal	Partly burned wood, sometimes used for forge fuel.
Clinch cutter	Tool for cutting nails, as in horseshoeing.

Clinker breaker	Device for clearing forge fire of clinkers.
Clinkers	Melted-out impurities in coal.
Coil steel	Usually, coil springs.
Coke	Partly burned coal or petroleum, used as fuel in blacksmithing.
Cold chisel	Chisel for cutting cold metal.
Countersink	To recess a hole.
Cross-peen hammer	Hammer with a blunt chisel back face ninety degrees to the handle.
Crystalline structure in metal	The pattern of particles that comprise a metal.
Cutting torch	Acetylene or LP gas/oxygen torch for cutting iron/steel.
Damascus steel	Pattern-welded, layered wrought iron and carbon steel.
Decalescence (point of)	Temperature at which steel molecules are in a state of flux, allowing hardening by quenching or sudden cooling.
Digging bar	Chisel-pointed steel bar.
"Draw a piece of iron"	Flatten, extend by heating and hammering; stretch.
Drawknife	Two-handled tool for shaving wood.
"Draw to a . . ."	Either flatten and extend metal by hammering, or heat to a given tempering color.
Drift out	Enlarge, as a hole.
Drifts	Tools for enlarging holes by punching.
Drill press	Stationary drilling machine.
Farrier	One who applies iron shoes to horses' feet.
Farrier vs. blacksmith	A farrier shoes horses. A blacksmith works iron/steel. Sometimes one does both.
Firebrick	Brick that withstands heat.
Firepot	Shaped center of the forge into which air is forced.
Flatter	Struck tool with handle, used to produce a flat, controlled surface on hot iron.
Flue	Chimney stack.
Flux	Substance, usually containing borax, to retard oxidation of heated iron/steel.
Forge	Container for fire to heat metal.
Forge weld	To join iron/steel by hammering while white hot.
Foundry	Operation for casting iron/steel.
Froe	Tool for splitting (riving) shakes or shingles.
Fuller	Two-piece tool, the bottom like a blunt hardy, top like a blunt cold chisel, with or without handle, used to shoulder or dent hot iron with more accuracy than the hammer peen.
Gas forge	Forge fed by gas and forced air.
Grain in metals	The elongated particles that make up the metal.

Grate	Device for holding fire, to let ashes fall through.
Hardy	Stationary chisel set into the hardy hole in an anvil.
Hardy hole	Square hole in face of anvil for holding tools.
Heat treating	Combination of hardening and tempering steels and other metals.
"Heeling the hammer"	Holding the handle at a low angle.
Hold an edge	Resist dulling.
Hone	Abrasive tool for sharpening.
Horn of the anvil	Rounded extension, used for working loops, curves.
Hot cut	Chisel used on hot metal.
"Hot short"	Tendency of some iron/steel to crumble when worked.
Iron	Relatively soft ferrous metal containing no carbon.
Jump weld	Forge weld made by butting the end of one piece into the side of another and hammering at white heat.
Lap scarf	The shape given ends of metal to be welded in an overlap.
Leaf spring	Vehicle spring comprised of layers.
Low sulfur	In coal, that containing little sulfur.
Machinist's vise	Vise that mounts on a tabletop.
Masonry forge	Forge set into brick or stone.
Maul	Large hammer, or chisel-pointed hammer for splitting wood.
Metallurgy	The study of metals.
Mild steel	That with little or no carbon content, which cannot be hardened.
Mill pick	Tool for dressing millstones.
Molten	Liquid state, as hot iron/steel.
Mushrooming	The spreading of a struck surface of a tool.
Normalize	To cool a heated metal in the air to its normal hardness.
Offset	Often, a double bend to create parallel but nonaligned sections of a shaft.
Oxidation scale	Thin flakes of oxidized metal, caused by heat.
Oxidize	To combine with oxygen, which produces scale in iron/steel.
Pan forge	A shallow forge with no firepot.
Peavy	Similar to a cant hook; a tool for handling logs.
Peter Wright	Patent anvil brand, English.
Pitting	Burning or oxidation causing cavities in the metal.
Pivot bolt	One that holds, but allows swiveling.
Pritchel hole	The round punch (pritchel) hole in the anvil face.
Prybar	Also pinch bar or wrecking bar. Bar with a hook and split chisel point at one end, straight with chisel at the other.
Punch	Tool for making holes in hot metal, or for pushing objects through holes.

Purlins	Timbers parallel to the ridge in a roof.
Pyrometer	High-temperature thermometer.
Quarry steel	That used for stone-cutting.
Quench	To harden by sudden immersion in liquid.
Ratchet blower	One driven by repeated engagement of a one-way, sliding lever.
Re-bar	Construction slang for reinforcing rod.
"Red short"	Same as "hot short." Tendency of some iron/steel to crumble when worked.
Reface (an anvil)	To resurface the top by welding on a plate of carbon steel.
Rive	To split, as in wooden shakes or shingles.
Rivet	To join pieces by flattening the ends of a short rod through holes in them.
Scale	Oxidized metal that forms in thin sheets from heat.
Scarfing	Shaping ends to be welded.
Scarf weld	Weld for which the components have been shaped.
Shear	In blacksmithing, a tool for cutting iron/steel.
Slack tub	Originally "slake." A tub for quenching or cooling hot metal.
Sledge (sled)	Simple vehicle for moving material, on runners.
Smith	The craftsperson who works metals.
Smithy	The shop in which the smith works.
Splitting maul	Chisel-pointed hammer for splitting wood.
Spring steel	Steel used for springs, of high carbon content.
Steel	Iron with carbon in it.
"Steel an axe"	To weld new steel onto the cutting edge.
Straight-peen hammer	Hammer with the blunt chisel back face parallel to the handle.
Sulfur	Substance found in coal.
Swage	Two-piece tool, the bottom to fit the anvil hardy hole, the top handled. Each has a shaped, matched groove, in which iron is shaped while hot.
Tang	Extended end of a tool for attaching a handle.
Tap and die	Nut-and-bolt threading tools.
Temper	To regulate hardness in metal by controlled heating, after hardening.
Temper-drawing	Tempering; taking quench hardness out to a desired degree by controlled heat. The second step in heat treating.
Tempering fluids	Those used in quenching; usually water, brine, or oil.
"Toeing the hammer"	Angling the handle too high.
Tongs	Gripping tool for holding hot metal.
Tool steel (carbon steel)	Steel of high carbon content used for tools to work other steel cold, or to work stone.

Tough steel versus brittle steel	Medium-carbon steel vs. high-carbon steel. The ability of the former to withstand breakage; the latter to withstand wear.
Trip-hammer	Powered hammer/anvil machine.
Trunnel	"Tree nail." Wooden peg used to hold timbers.
Tuyere	Shaped air blast into forge firepot.
Upset	To thicken by hammering into a mass, as opposed to stretching, as in drawing out.
Vise (stump or tree)	Also blacksmith's vise or leg vise. Holding device with a long leg anchored below for extra stability.
Whetstone	Stone for sharpening tools.
Wrought iron	Soft iron and silica, very fibrous, now rare.

Index

Illustrations noted **bold**.